CONCORD
and the Dawn of
REVOLUTION

CONCORD
and the Dawn of
REVOLUTION
The Hidden Truths

D. MICHAEL RYAN

THE
History
PRESS

Published by The History Press
Charleston, SC 29403
www.historypress.net

Cover image: Lieutenant Colonel Smith's column of Regulars under attack on all sides by the provincials during the April 19, 1775 march back from Concord to Boston with flankers moving out for protection. *Retreat from Lexington and Concord* by A. Lassell Ripley (1886–1969). Reproduced by permission of the Paul Revere Life Insurance Company.

First published 2007
Second printing 2008

Manufactured in the United States
ISBN 978.1.59629.186.7

Library of Congress Cataloging-in-Publication Data

Ryan, D. Michael, 1944-
Concord and the dawn of revolution : the hidden truths / D. Michael Ryan.
p. cm.
ISBN 978-1-59629-186-7 (alk. paper)
1. Concord, Battle of, Concord, Mass., 1775. 2. Concord, Battle of, Concord, Mass., 1775--Anecdotes. 3. Lexington, Battle of, Lexington, Mass., 1775. 4. Lincoln (Mass.)--History, Military--18th century. 5. United States--History--Revolution, 1775-1783--Causes. 6. Massachusetts--History--Revolution, 1775-1783--Anecdotes. 7. United States--History--Revolution, 1775-1783--Anecdotes. I. Title.
E241.C7R93 2007
973.3'311--dc22
2006032911

CONTENTS

Acknowledgements	7
Introduction: The Truth of It	11
Haunted and Heroic: The Hartwell Family	21
Recognizing the Enemy Within: Daniel Bliss, Tory	30
A Tale of Two Families: Joined by Love, Shattered by War	35
James Barrett: A Patriot's Name for Posterity	42
Espionage, Spies and Intrigue Surround Concord	49
A Place of Honor: Charles Miles in Extraordinary Times	56
Whatever Can Go Wrong Will Go Wrong	61
An Unfurled Flag and the Concord Fight	70
Tragic Act Begets Revenge and Propaganda	79
Joseph Thaxter: Minister of the Lord at the Bridge	84
Legacy of the Daughters of Liberty	89
A Matter of Color: Slaves and the Two Fights for Freedom	97
Support from Our British "Cousins"	105
Intolerable Papists Influence a Revolution	111
Irksome Concord Jail and a Parliamentarian Prisoner	118
About the Author	125

Acknowledgements

I dedicate this book to the memory of my mom, Gertrude M. (Boisvert) Ryan (1924–1988), and dad, Leland G. "Duke" Ryan (1919–1997); to my beloved sisters, Marion M. Ryan and Diana L. Crowley; to the wonderful love of my life, Goddaughter Kathryn "Kate" Squillace; and to my true love and soul mate, Kate Shannon.

People very important to my research, writing and publishing and who deserve recognition include Leslie Perrin Wilson, curator/archivist for the Special Collections, Concord Free Public Library, who graciously welcomed me into her mystical world of sources and tolerated my intellectual wanderings; Terry Wallace, archivist, Minute Man National Historical Park (MMNHP), Concord, Massachusetts; Lucille Daniel Stott, former editor of the *Concord Journal* who first allowed me the space to be published; and Debbie Bier, editor of on-line *Concord Magazine*, a Concord history cohort, supporter and publisher. Special friends along the way include Brad Bigham, who convinced me Concord *should be* "home"; Doris Decker Hancock, who reminds me always that Gloucester *is* "home"; and Christine Squillace, who *makes* Gloucester "home" and shares Kate.

I am a strong believer that historical research and knowledge are not for an individual or just for publication but should be shared through public interpretation, reenacting and programming at historical sites. To this end, Superintendent Nancy Nelson and Rangers (current and past) Lou Sideris, Jim Hollister, Bob Derry, Tom Casey, Margie/Peg Hicks, Jessica Liptak, Mark Nichipor and numerous great "seasonals" have supported and indulged me in the use of Minute Man National Historical Park to perform and bring my material to the people. Their "work" is seen throughout this book.

Like the U.S. Army, being in the "reenacting community" is akin to having another family that you may be separated from occasionally but never leave.

Every spring the start of another season is like a family reunion. To my American, French, British, Loyalist and Prussian/German cohorts, thank you from the bottom of my heart for a grand thirty years with more to come. Your value to the public and our nation's history cannot be overemphasized! The Concord and Lincoln Minute Men (LMM) have humored me as their historian for many years, and I have been greatly blessed with a kindred spirit, historian, educator, friend and reenactor in Dr. Don Hafner of Boston College and the LMM.

Special thanks also to my "in-laws" within the Guild of Historic Interpreters, who continue to amaze and bring the eighteenth- and nineteenth-century worlds to the public in new and exciting ways. And finally, thanks to the Jolly Rogues—Jim Murray, Al Hicks, Paul Harty, Herb Broadbent—and the Ladies Remembered—Peg Hicks and Joyce Murray—for allowing me a musical "family" outlet in which to enjoy life and escape reality occasionally. "Peace through Music!"

Contributing directly to this book, worthy of note and without whom the final product would not have been so excellent, I must recognize and thank Jenny Kaemmerlen, commissioning editor at The History Press, who offered me this opportunity and then suffered my constant e-mails; Dennis Dostie, whose volunteer photography for the MMNHP brings the world of us reenactors to life, and has done the same for my articles; Richard Stevenson, an excellent photographer, friend and cohort on many a project; Colonel Vincent J-R Kehoe, *the* expert on the eighteenth-century British military in North America, founder of the re-created Tenth Regiment of Foot and my history "godfather"; Aryeh Finklestein, a fellow researcher, dear friend and Ammi White expert; Guild of Historic Interpreters members Beverly and Kelly Malone and our favorite King's Regular, the "highly decorated" Graeme Marsden; Concordant Volunteers Adam and Evan Hodges-LeClaire, Lauren Stern, Anna Ohalezky; Sharon Speildenner, librarian, Beverly Historical Society and Museum; Meghan Maceiko, marketing, Paul Revere Corporation; Kathy Young, university archivist, Special Collections–Cudahy Library, Loyola University Chicago; Doreen Stevens, museum administrator, Arlington Historical Society.

Finally, gracious platitudes to Graeme Marsden for volunteering his valuable time to proofread and edit this work with his English/British perspective and outstanding command of His/Her Majesty's English! And humble kudos to Doris Hancock for her proofreading and editing from an English teacher's perspective, which included the guiding spirits of Claudia and Charlotte from Gloucester High School days.

Thanks to you all for making this book and my life special events!

We are sometimes made aware of a kindness long passed, and realize that there have been times when our Friends' thoughts of us were so pure and lofty a character that they passed over us like the winds of heaven unnoticed; when they treated us not as what we were, but as what we aspired to be.

—Henry David Thoreau, 1849

INTRODUCTION
The Truth of It

Exactly what is historic truth? Can it be found? What resources and materials exist to support any perception of what is true? Can historians attain absolute objectivity and accuracy? And if so, can good, interesting history still be had, despite trendy doubts?

Just what is this truth that seems to be so ardently sought by many? Defined, it means actual fact, conformity to reality, verifiable indisputable fact, genuine, actual existence, freedom from deceit. Truth is momentary and it is eternal. It must be looked for in primary source materials (original letters, diaries, accounts, records) as can be found in such locations as the Special Collections of the Concord Free Public Library (a singularly unique holding of local historic materials) and the Massachusetts Historical Society.

An event must be studied within the context of its own time and participants. Historical truth is for the purist seeking unadulterated fact, not revisionism or popular myth. Since the 1880s and especially in the past half-century, searching for historic truth has become as much scientific endeavor as scholarly research. This is in great part due to new wondrous means of locating and examining sites and artifacts. Computers have had a great impact on how research is conducted. But can the historic truth of any event or person *really* be found?

A challenging aspect for any historian addressing a past event or an epoch can be writing, all the while knowing the outcome, and trying to ignore that in telling the true story. Yet by not putting the future out of mind when writing about the past, what is being composed can be tainted.

Francis Bacon wrote, "It is the true office of history to represent the events themselves, together with the counsels, and to leave the observations and conclusions thereupon to the liberty and faculty of everyone's judgment." But is this the reality of history? Henry David Thoreau noted, "It is the province of the historian to find out, not what was, but what is." St. Augustine reminded us that with any historic event, there exists the actual occurrence, followed by how it lingers in memory and is embellished by our experiences (and recordings).

History and memory are indelibly linked, and hence the science of the latter must be understood. Depositions or writings may be accomplished days, months or years after an event, and thus possibly affected by time, age, willful forgetting or purposeful remembering, memory loss or values of the recollector. Too often the writer or storyteller may "construct" the event rather than "recall" it. There exists private or individual memory of an event, and public or social, community and national remembrance of the same event, all of which can differ.

In his 1835 journal, Ralph Waldo Emerson addressed his fascination at what is preserved of history, "a few anecdotes of moral quality of some momentary act or word," while ignoring more important "laws, expeditions, books and kingdoms." In his essay *History*, he writes, "All inquiry into antiquity…is the desire to do away with the there and then and introduce in its place the here and now…The student interprets the age of chivalry by his own age of chivalry…by quite parallel miniature experiences of his own… All history is subjective."

Henry David Thoreau in an 1841 journal entry noted, "Nothing so restores and humanizes antiquity…and makes it blithe…as the discovery of some natural sympathy between it and the present…The Heavens stood over the heads of our ancestors as near as to us." There does exist a strong desire to connect a historic event to the present and to us personally. But while historians may always be rewriting history, the past in fact cannot be revised, for what happened, happened. Should history be subjective?

Within days of the April 19, 1775 events in Lexington and Concord, the Provincial Congress established committees to compose a "Narrative of the Excursion and Ravages of the King's Troops" and to gather eyewitness depositions to "authenticate as soon as possible…to prove and elucidate the truth of facts related thereof." From the start, truth was purveyed both by Dr. Benjamin Church, a traitor, and by depositions that seemed not necessarily individual, accurate, eyewitness accounts of events, but instead statements in answer to prescribed, subjective questions often attested to by multiple men. The purpose of this project was to produce propaganda aimed at gaining popular support in England for the colonial cause. In such an environment began the truth and history of April 19.

Even Concord's beloved Reverend Dr. Ezra Ripley, in penning his 1827 *History of the Fight at Concord* to support his town's pivotal role in beginning the Revolution, appears to have pressed old veterans at local taverns in seeking confirmation of his personal views, while ignoring facts such as the important role of Acton's Isaac Davis and his minute company. Yet Ripley claimed to write "a fair and current statement of facts" since "nations of the earth are interested in the American Revolution…and circumstances of the actual commencement" and thus "it is our aim to give them correct information." Unfortunately, available information is often overlooked or ignored, and when the end justifies the means in writing history, truth may not out.

Dr. David Hackett Fischer in his excellent *Paul Revere's Ride* (1994) presents an appendix, "Historiography—Myths After the Midnight Ride," in which the subject is examined over various periods in America's history, explaining how each myth was accomplished in order to meet the needs of the specific epoch. Of interest is how Revere himself and his 1775 actions were presented relative to particular junctures in our history, such as "The Union in Crisis: Longfellow's Myth of the Lone Rider"; "Myths for Imperial America: Colonel Revere as a Man on Horseback"; "An Age of Disbelief: The Myths of the American Debunkers"; "Crusade for Democracy: The Myth of the Common Man"; "The Cold War: The Myth of the Capitalist Democracy"; "The Age of Vietnam: The Myth of the Evil America"; and "Academic History: Political Correctness and Paul Revere."

Details surrounding the Concord Fight may be found in an ever-increasing body of historical literature from the 1775 Amos Doolittle engravings; 1824–27 participant depositions aimed at supporting either Concord or Lexington as the location where hostilities began and shots were first fired; 1830–70 various town histories; and 1875 centennial writings that continued the Concord-Lexington debate on primacy and introduced the Bedford Flag issue; to 1920s post–World War I revisionist histories, many of which purposefully sought to downplay any glory of war; 1940s and 1950s books offering fresh research; bicentennial writings (many of questionable substance or research); and the recent myriad of publications adding to the resurgence of interest in the American Revolution.

Recent authors of note who have shed new or different light on the April 19 story and other related events include Frank Warren Coburn, who conducted new research and actually visited historic sites; Harold Murdock, who questioned existing theories and facts and introduced new ones; Allen French, who visited archives in England to find primary sources and reviewed Gage's collected papers; Arthur Tourtellot, who placed April 19 into historic context;

Vincent J-R Kehoe, who traveled to England and intimately studied the British military, its circumstances and point of view; Robert A. Gross, who moved to and lived in Concord and brought a social perspective and context to the issues; and David Hackett Fischer, who did new original research (1994), rekindled interest in April 19 and became a researcher's guide.

As a local historian involved in the eighteenth-century colonial period, and specifically the beginnings of the American Revolution, I toil to locate the ancient, real truth of activities and people on and surrounding April 19, 1775, and then understand how they relate to the present. I am aware of the pitfalls after having observed the revisionism of historical events that I witnessed, such as the 1960s civil rights marches in the South, the division of Berlin from West Germany and the Berlin Wall, the Woodstock concert, the anti-war movement and the Vietnam conflict. While I understand and allow my experiences to help interpret and appreciate the past, I do not permit them to create the past. With this in mind, I spend countless hours reading, researching and then standing at historic sites, contemplating the events that took place there. As much as can be possible, I attempt to infuse my consciousness with some of the original mindset and viewpoints of the participants, in an attempt to better reach the truth of it.

An example has been my study of what may actually have occurred during the meeting of officers and town leaders above North Bridge on April 19, 1775, just before the fight. Aside from the decision to have Isaac Davis and his Acton minute company lead the march, what caused the hesitant leaders to choose the option of marching into the center of town or die in the attempt? Many believed it to be the reported heroic words of young Adjutant Lieutenant Joseph Hosmer, who upon seeing smoke rising from Concord is reported to have exclaimed, "Will you let them burn the town down?" However, it seems that much more in terms of words, attitudes, purposes and personalities were involved both in Hosmer's comments and in the officers' decision making.

The same can be said regarding Davis's often used quote, "I haven't a man who is afraid to go." The actual wording, context and reasons for the statement are much more fascinating. The Concord Fight at North Bridge is an example of primary source materials often being shunned in order to foster a particular point of view, a specific agenda (glory, nation-defining, self-importance for an individual town) or a timely value or ideal. The fact and fiction of and surrounding this military encounter have taken on epic proportions over the years, and each might fill a year-long course of study in a college.

History often reflects the time in which it is written, versus the time in which it occurred. Hence the criminal destruction of taxed tea later becomes "the Tea Party," the firing on an unruly mob in defense leads to "the Boston Massacre" and skirmishes at Lexington and Concord are termed "Battles." The naming of an event often reflects a cause, value, political view, propaganda or personal bent. Historic events placed in such a current context are "presentist history," usually the product of revisionism with a purpose. Unfortunately this often leads to a homogenized, simple to understand, politically correct story that is devoid of much reality.

Though history is supposed to be about truth, we have numerous materials and writings that since 1775 have created and supported myth, embellishment, personal belief, current conception and even outright falsehood concerning the early days of the American Revolution. Perhaps this is due to what historian Carl Becker notes as history acting as an artificial extension of social memory and is thus imperfect and selective in its reconstruction. While outright fiction or historic fiction may be entertaining, truth and factual occurrences are more often than not just as much so. At least the former should be qualified and identified for what they are in actuality, as with *Concord Bridge* by Howard Horne, 1952; *April Morning* by Howard Fast, 1961; and my *Jonas Bateman's Letters August 1774–May 1775*, a series in the *Concord Journal*, August 1999–May 2000.

All this having been said, now the question arises, "Who cares?" While purists desire truth and accuracy, does the public? Do you? Does it matter? Or do individuals want to believe what has been told to them through school, books or movies, the stories that make them comfortable, the "truth" that supports personal beliefs? Can we ever really know the "truth" of historic events, times or people? Was an activity such as the fight at Concord's North Bridge as important locally, nationally or internationally then as it appears to be now, or is it a figment of our present historical imagination as to its place in the scheme of history? As with any trip where the journey is often as important as the destination, so it is with the seeking of historic truth.

Thus, Samuel Hoar's 1824 "first forcible resistance" (later used by Dr. Edward Jarvis for Concord's Battle Monument, dedicated 1837) and Ralph Waldo Emerson's 1836 "shot heard round the world" ("Concord Hymn") will reflect, as they were originally intended to, ideas and values. However, they also will be read and understood as providing support for a town's important place in the start of a Revolution and/or as specific, physical acts (that is, unfurling a flag).

And for better or for worse, our history will include fact, myth, reality, folk tales and oral traditions. And as new evidence appears or views are altered in light of current events, history will be rewritten. Two old sayings remind us that those who fail to learn from history are bound to repeat it, and it is important to know where we came from in order to understand where we are and where we are going. Thus my goals in studying, recreating, interpreting, researching and writing history are to be as accurate and true to fact as possible, debunking myths when appropriate.

Please read this collection of stories and decide where the truth and its importance lie, especially if past beliefs are challenged. Inquiry, conversation and the seeking of knowledge and truth are important—but only the reader can decide to what degree.

Irrefutable facts will stand forever, and I, like other historian Galahads before, will continue the quest for the Holy Grail of historic truth, wherever it may lead, always hoping by such to find new perspectives and information in support of it.

Bailyn, Bernard. *On the Teaching and Writing of History*. Hanover, NH: Union Press of New England, 1994.

Fischer, David Hackett. *Paul Revere's Ride*. New York: Oxford University Press, 1994.

Kammen, Michael. *In the Past Lane: Historical Perspective on American Culture*. New York: Oxford University Press, 1997.

Ryan, D. Michael. "To Support the Truth of It," an oration at the exhibit opening to commemorate the 225th anniversary of the Concord Fight, sponsored by the Trustees of the Concord Free Public Library, April 7, 2000.

Young, Alfred F. *The Shoemaker and the Tea Party*. Boston: Beacon Press, 1999.

HAUNTED AND HEROIC
The Hartwell Family

Hartwells have lived along the Bay Road in Concord and Lincoln, Massachusetts, near the Lexington border since the latter part of the seventeenth century. This thoroughfare served as a main route from Boston to westward towns and settlements such as Albany, New York; New Hampshire; and even Canada. By the time of hostilities with Great Britain in 1775, a section of the road fourteen miles from Boston, in the north district of Lincoln, contained two Hartwell dwellings. To the east was located the house of William Smith, captain of the town's minute company.

In the westernmost home lived Ephraim and Elizabeth Hartwell, with their five young children. Between October 5 and 27, 1740, all five youngsters died of "throat distemper." Believed to be diphtheria or scarlet fever, this highly contagious disease usually attacked those under the age of ten. The symptoms included fever, a cough, sore throat and weakness. Treatments at the time were minimal and in some instances, horrific. Isaac, age eleven months, passed away on the fifth; John, age three years eleven months, on the seventh; Ephraim, age six years eleven months, on the ninth; Samuel, age five years six months, on the eleventh; and Elizabeth, age one year ten months, on the twenty-seventh. Thus began the epic odyssey of a preeminent family of both Concord and Lincoln, whose members would be heroically involved in revolutionary events while continuing to be haunted by tragic deaths.

Elizabeth and Ephraim face an empty home in early November 1740 following the sudden deaths of their five young children. *Photograph by Dennis Dostie, MMNHP volunteer.*

Ephraim Hartwell married Elizabeth Heywood (both descendants of early Concord settlers) on November 7, 1732. With the early exodus of three older brothers, he remained to care for his father, whose estate he inherited and who provided the land on which to build a homestead in 1733. The Hartwells quickly set about raising a family, understanding that children were the poor man's wealth, especially for farmers. By 1740 five babies had been born in six years. The husband and father provided for his wife and young ones working as a cordwainer (shoemaker) and farmer while also operating a small cider mill.

While eighteenth-century life was often hard and demanding, with death at an early age not unusual or unexpected, the sudden, swift loss of an entire family of children in 1740 had to be devastating for Elizabeth and Ephraim. Yet with faith in God, they began a second family in 1741 and over the next thirteen years produced nine more children (Elizabeth, Samuel, Abigail, Ephraim, John, Mary, Sarah, Isaac and Jonas). Mother Elizabeth had been with child when daughter Elizabeth died on October 27, and in loving memory named the newborn Elizabeth. It was not uncommon at the time for the names of deceased children to be passed to a newborn, and such occurred with the Hartwells.

With so large a brood, and the need for more space and income, Ephraim expanded his house and in 1756 obtained a license to operate an inn and tavern. It was not an easy task, requiring an application process that included a review of character by the town selectmen in their capacity as the licensing authority. It also necessitated the prospective innkeeper being able to provide food and overnight accommodations for travelers and animals. Ephraim met all requirements, especially in character, for he had military experience (rank of cornet) and had served as a selectman. Additionally, he came from an established family and was involved in the founding of Lincoln during its 1754 separation from Concord.

By 1775, the oldest Hartwell son, Samuel, was residing alongside his father in the family patriarch William's 1690s homestead with his wife, Mary, and three very young daughters. As conflict with England seemed imminent, he and his brother John, already members of the militia, volunteered in January to join the newly established Lincoln minute company, and were duly elected sergeants by their peers. Brother Isaac was a private in the unit that was commanded by Bay Road neighbor Captain William Smith. The early morning hours of April 19 would bring fear, danger and uncertainty to the Hartwell family.

At near 1:30 a.m. alarm rider Dr. Samuel Prescott banged on Ephraim's tavern door, announcing that British Regulars were on the road to Concord. A servant girl (referred to in oral tradition as Sukey but more likely named Violet, as cited in Ephraim's will) was sent scurrying next door to Samuel's house with the urgent message, but she was too terrified to go farther with the news. While her husband and his brothers prepared to muster, tradition records that Mary handed baby Lucy (four months) to the servant and ran into the night to Captain Smith's house to deliver him the alarm. Later in the morning after watching the Redcoat column march past her door, and fearing for the welfare of her children (and the Hartwell men and others gathered at Concord), she fled a distance to her father's house for safety. Samuel, John and Isaac (and possibly Jonas with the Lincoln militia) stood at North Bridge in Concord and then participated in the pursuit of the king's troops to Charlestown. Their brother Ephraim, who lived farther west in Princeton, Massachusetts, responded to the alarm as a private in that town's militia company under Captain Boaz Moore.

The Hartwell brothers each later served various lengths of time in the military. Samuel was a regimental quartermaster at the Battle of White

Jonas and John, sons in the "second" Hartwell family, tend livestock at the Lincoln farm in 1776. *Photograph by Dennis Dostie, MMNHP volunteer.*

Plains, New York, and was discharged in 1779. John was a militia company lieutenant and captain. Isaac served as a sergeant in John's unit and by 1778–79 had risen to the rank of lieutenant. Jonas also served as a sergeant in John's company before entering Harvard College in 1776, although he may also have served during his student days. In 1777 when John became ill, he went on leave from the army, settled back in the Hartwell family house on the Bay Road in Lincoln and assumed operational responsibility for his father's tavern until 1787. Ephraim served as a quartermaster and adjutant, returned to Princeton and rose to the rank of captain in the Massachusetts Militia.

The Hartwell children continued to be prominent citizens, prospered and added new generations to the population, but tragedy still haunted them. Ephraim's oldest child, Elizabeth, married Lieutenant Jonas Stratton of Concord on September 3, 1764. By 1769 the couple had moved to New Ipswich, New Hampshire, and then to Alexandria, New Hampshire, where in 1774 Jonas was struck and killed by a falling tree while clearing land. Elizabeth and her children, Lydia and Jonas, then returned to Lincoln briefly and on May 24, 1778, she married Continental army officer Enoch Putnam of Danvers, Massachusetts, who rose to the rank of colonel in 1782. After his death in 1792, Elizabeth returned to New Ipswich, where she passed away on June 2, 1823.

The Hartwells' youngest daughter Sarah was married on December 28, 1772, to the Reverend Jacob Bigelow, who had been ordained the Gospel minister in Sudbury on November 11 of the same year. Sadly, she died suddenly on August 21, 1773, during childbirth at the age of twenty-three. Her sister Abigail, who was named for the paternal grandmother, married Jonas Jones on September 6, 1763, and moved to Shrewsbury, Massachusetts, then to New Ipswich—a popular Hartwell resettlement location—and died in 1809 at age sixty-five. Her husband, who at the age of ten accompanied his father to Crown Point in the French and Indian War (1746), lived into his eighty-first year before falling from his horse in a fatal 1817 accident.

The youngest Hartwell child, Jonas, the only one born (June 26, 1754) in the newly established town of Lincoln two months after the first town meeting, had a most interesting life that came to a tragic, strange and intriguing end in a foreign land. The only family member to gain a higher education, he attended Harvard College, entering in 1776—the year the institution returned to Cambridge from its sojourn in Concord. In November he recorded the first of what became an unusual number of leaves of absence for "nervous disorders" throughout his student days. When General William Prescott signed a June 1779 letter of explanation related to a previous medical/mental episode, it raised the possibility that perhaps Jonas was actually away on military service (from December 1776 to March 1777 he was listed on muster rolls). His absentee problems (and a greatly overdue library book) aside, he was allowed to graduate in June and then continue studies that led to a master's degree in 1782.

Within several years of departing Harvard, Jonas had become a very successful international Boston merchant. The war for independence had ended and America had begun searching for identity and its place in the world. While in Bilbao, Spain, conducting business and marketing a cargo of tobacco, he was suddenly arrested and imprisoned in Leon by order of the Holy Inquisition. His "crime" was apparently being "so imprudent and unguarded as to express himself with some contempt relative to their Religion [Catholicism]." One of his ship captains sped back to Massachusetts with the news, and within weeks (February 24, 1785) Governor Thomas Cushing reported the incident and petitioned Congress for assistance in obtaining Hartwell's release. The new American government's Secretary for Foreign Affairs John Jay referred the case on March 7 for inquiry and factual investigation to his Charge des Affaires William Carmichael in Spain. He in turn contacted the Spanish Foreign Minister Jose Monino, Conde de Florida Blanca and also made a report (on February 27) to Benjamin Franklin, senior American diplomat in Europe (France) on the matter. Jay reported back to Congress (March 18; No. 65, 11, folio 265).

The Spanish minister was sympathetic to the American request and Hartwell's plight, as he had a personal interest in curbing the inquisitor general's powers. However, the American Congress on March 19 noted that it could not object to Hartwell's being tried and treated agreeably to the laws of Spain for crimes committed there. It also stated that if imprisonment were the consequence for violation of Spanish law, an application by United States officials for liberation would be not as a matter of right but of favor. The obligation of secrecy on this correspondence was waived in order that its contents could be shared by the foreign secretary with the Massachusetts delegate, who in turn might then present it to Jonas's father, Ephraim.

Unfortunately all of this governmental, bureaucratic, diplomatic foot-dragging undermined Jonas's cause. In fact, according to the family, he died on March 2, 1785, supposedly of slow poisoning (food or drink) while in prison. Carmichael, in a letter to Franklin dated April 4, 1785, mentioned the "death of Mr. [Jonas] Hartwell at a moment when he would certainly have had his liberty."

The family then began the arduous task of making arrangements for an executor to settle and close Hartwell's financial, business and personal affairs in Spain. The process continued well into October 1786 and involved his father Ephraim, his brother John and his brother-in-law Enoch Putnam (a retired colonel, a Danvers, Massachusetts selectman and friend of a state delegate to Congress). Thus concluded the final sad chapter in the lives of the Hartwell family children.

Ephraim and Elizabeth lived to experience all of these events—heroics and tragedies—as he died on May 7, 1793, at age eighty-seven and she died on June 9, 1808, at age ninety-four. They had survived the loss of one family, the birth of another, a Revolution, untimely deaths and hardships, but at least in their final years the Hartwells were able to enjoy peace with many grandchildren and great-grandchildren. Haunted and heroic, they left a family legacy that continues as an intriguing part of the town histories in Concord and Lincoln.

NOTE: The Minute Man National Historical Park, National Park Service, obtained and restored the Ephraim Hartwell Tavern in the years 1979–1981 and the neighboring William Smith House in 1975–1983 (Route 2A, Lincoln). These historic structures are open seasonally to the public, and often brought to life with historic interpretations. The Samuel Hartwell house was operated for many years as a restaurant, then tragically destroyed in a 1968 fire, and only the remains of its superstructure-protected center chimney may be seen today.

Densmore, Lyman W. *Handbook of the Hartwell Genealogy, 1836–1887, An Account of the Descendents of William Hartwell of Concord, Massachusetts*. Little Rock, AR: Higginson Book Company, 1887.

Hartwell, John. *The Hartwells of America: A Genealogy*. Little Rock, AR: Higginson Book Company, 1956.

Hersey, Frank W.C. *Heroes of the Battle Road 1775*. Boston: Imprinted by Perry Walton, 1930.

Hicks, Marjorie. "The Hartwell Family." Unpublished paper. Concord, MA: Minute Man National Historical Park, October 2002.

Holten, Samuel, to William Carmichael. "Century of Lawmaking for a New Nation: U.S. Congressional Documents and Debates 1774–1875." 22. November 1, 1784, to November 6, 1785, papers, Library of Congress, 2003 (online).

MacLean, John C. *A Rich Harvest: The History, Buildings and People of Lincoln, Massachusetts*. Portsmouth, NH: Lincoln Historical Society, Peter E. Randall, publisher, 1987.

Malcolm, Joyce Lee. "The Scene of the Battle 1775—Historic Grounds Report, Cultural Resources Study 15." Boston: National Park Service, U.S. Department of the Interior, Minute Man National Historical Park, 1985.

Mulhern, Christopher H., and Orville W. Carroll. "Historic Structure Report—Architectural Data Section on the Hartwell Tavern." Concord, MA: National Park Service, U.S. Department of the Interior, Minute Man National Historical Park, 1975.

Recognizing the Enemy Within
Daniel Bliss, Tory

In 1774, it could be safely stated that few Tories resided within Concord. Yet one prominent supporter of the king was at the heart of a well-known family's division and had great influence upon events of April 19, 1775.

Daniel Bliss, Esquire, was the son of Reverend Daniel Bliss, minister of Concord's First Parish Church, and Mrs. Phebe (Walker) Bliss. Siblings included Thomas Theodore, who would become an officer in the American army and who was captured during Benedict Arnold's 1775–76 Quebec expedition; Samuel, who became a British army captain; Joseph, a staunch Whig who served in General Henry Knox's artillery unit and later as a captain and Continental army paymaster; and Phebe, who married her father's two successors—Reverend William Emerson, who served as an American army chaplain and gave his life in such service in October 1776, and following his death, Reverend Ezra Ripley.

A 1760 Harvard College graduate (Scholar of the House and on scholarship), Daniel developed a notable law practice in Rutland, Vermont, being appointed a justice of the peace in 1767, and was a comfortable conservative and "ardent supporter of precedent and establishment." In 1766 he married Isabel (Isabella) Murray, the daughter of aristocratic former British army colonel John Murray, the wealthiest man in Rutland. They returned to Concord in 1772 and lived in a home on the Milldam (current Walden Street).

The squire acted the aristocrat and his political views were very well known, yet his townsmen continually elected him to positions of importance, due to respect for his education, energy and abilities. He was said to have been brilliant, witty, a powerful public speaker, a scholar, a clear and logical thinker and a possessor of spotless integrity. In December 1772, he served on a committee to draft instructions for Concord's General Court representative Captain (later to be Colonel) James Barrett, who was on his way to the Boston assembly. Consensus held that Barrett should reflect Concord's loyalty to the king while noting concern over unconstitutional infringement of colonial rights and the payment to and influencing of judges by the Crown. Bliss refused to sign the committee report, as he would also do relative to future liberal, seditious documents, including the 1774 League and Solemn Covenant that prohibited all British imports to Massachusetts until the port of Boston was reopened and the Intolerable Acts rescinded. Yet he did at one point sign a testimonial letter regretting the departure from Boston of Royal Governor Thomas Hutchinson who had appointed Daniel a justice of the peace in Middlesex County.

Bliss further incited discontent in March 1773 by composing the epitaph for former slave John Jack's gravestone (still at the Hill Burying Ground), the words of which were later published in London, disparaging the liberty-loving Patriots for moral hypocrisy in owning slaves while steadfastly refusing to become slaves themselves to Great Britain. In part he wrote, "God wills us free, man wills us slaves. I will as God wills, God's will be done...Tho' he lived in a land of liberty, he lived a slave." Bliss believed that personal freedom was a God-given right of humanity and that slavery had no place.

The exasperation of his townsmen continued. Speaking in Concord at the August 30–31, 1774 Middlesex County Convention, Bliss exhorted his fellow citizens in a sarcastic tone to support the king and royal governor, while setting aside their futile, childish opposition to the parent nation, a stand that he said could only end in disaster. He further warned of the folly of resisting the might of the British Empire. Fellow Concordian Joseph Hosmer, in response, spoke eloquently of love for family and home, and of liberties hard earned over generations, all of which should not be taken away by strangers or distant temporal powers. Bliss, once a legal aide to Governor Hutchinson, lost the debate and would soon cause his patriotic father-in-law Reverend William Emerson to note, "Verily, our enemies are of our own household."

Events moved swiftly. Concord hosted the October 1774 Provincial Congress gathering, became a depot for military stores and weapons, formed two of the newly required minute companies and had its militia drilling more often. By February 1775 British Regulars raided Salem, Massachusetts, attempting to capture cannon. Bliss, more blatant in his Tory ways than ever, hosted two British spies—Ensign Henry De Berniere and Captain John Brown (first name questionable)—on March 20. These men, on a mission

Bliss meets with Gage's spies, providing lists and pointing out the location of provincial military supplies and weapons in Concord. *Photograph by Richard Stevenson.*

to obtain information on the Rebels' militia training, geography between Boston and Concord and the location of cannon and military materials, were found out immediately by their clothing and their "English" mannerisms. Yet Bliss, "a friend to government," blatantly welcomed them to his house for supper and provided detailed accounts and locations of all weapons (including twelve cannon) and supplies in town.

Bliss knew that a county committee was systematically visiting homes of suspected Tories, his guests' identity had been discovered and his life had been threatened. Thus fearing for his safety, he departed Concord for Boston as a guide for and under the protection of the spies. He would never return home. In early April, with the help of brother Samuel, several family members along with personal valuables were reunited with him in Boston. Most likely he met at some point with the new Royal Governor, General Thomas Gage, to confirm the reports of colonial traitor and spy Dr. Benjamin Church.

Bliss remained unmolested in Boston until the further outbreak of hostilities, when he and his family decided to hastily sail to Quebec, a letter of introduction in hand from Gage to Sir Guy Carleton. A miserable winter with no money or credit followed, and during the invasion of fortress Quebec by colonials Colonel Benedict Arnold and Brigadier General Richard Montgomery, Bliss manned the walls as a private sentinel. It was during this campaign that his brother Thomas Theodore, serving in the provincial militia ranks, was captured and imprisoned for the remainder of the war.

Following the British victory at Quebec, Bliss was appointed assistant commissary-general with the rank of colonel. His brother-in-law Reverend Emerson, serving as chaplain with the American army at Fort Ticonderoga in September 1776, attempted to write him but the letter would not or could not be delivered. In 1777 Bliss accompanied General John Burgoyne on his ill-fated trek toward Saratoga, New York, and history. But fever resulted in his return to Quebec prior to the September/October battles and the defeat that led ultimately to surrender of the northern British army.

At war's end in 1783, Bliss settled in Belmont near Fredericton, New Brunswick, Canada, and became a very successful lawyer and judge, headed the New Brunswick bar, served as a member of His Majesty's Council and also as chief justice of the Court of Common Pleas. He even sent an envoy to an old friend and adversary, American General Henry Knox, asking that an accompanying letter and money be delivered to his ailing mother. Knox graciously obliged.

Bliss's Concord home was the only Loyalist property in town confiscated by the Commissioners of Estates of Conspirators and Absentees, under the Massachusetts 1778 Act of Sequestration. Following a November 1780 trial in absentia at which he was found guilty of "levying war and conspiracy to levy war against the Government and people of this Province, Colony and State," his property was sold at auction on March 6, 1781, for 278 pounds, 2 shillings, 10 pence to be used in funding the war effort.

Though he never wrote to any relatives in Massachusetts other than his mother during or after the war, Bliss did visit the state, and might have resettled there, had he been willing to undergo the indignity of an appeal to his trial and a successful overturning of the decision.

Bliss passed away at his home in Belmont in 1806, leaving his estate to son John Murray Bliss, himself a lawyer, solicitor general and judge, commander in chief and administrator for New Brunswick and, during the War of 1812, commander of the provincial militia. Thus ended the saga of Concord's most notorious Loyalist whose life and family influenced not only the events of April 19, 1775, but also their town's history for many years. Had they not been Tories, perhaps Daniel and his sons were just the type of gentlemen the young republic could have used to build and advance into the future.

Bliss, John Hosmer. *Genealogy of the Bliss Family in America from about the Year 1550 to 1880*. Boston: original by author, 1881.

Harris, John. *American Rebels*. Boston: Boston Globe Newspaper Company, 1974.

Scudder, Townsend. *Concord: American Town*. Boston: Little, Brown and Company, 1947.

Tolman, George. *John Jack, The Slave and Daniel Bliss, The Tory*. Concord, MA: Patriot Press, 1902.

Transcripts of the ancient records of Concord. Special Collections, Concord Free Public Library.

Wheeler, Ruth R. *Concord: Climate for Freedom*. Yarmouthport, MA: Printing and Publishing Production Associates, 1967.

A Tale of Two Families
Joined by Love, Shattered by War

As Tuesday, April 18, 1775, drew to a close, Dr. Samuel Prescott (age twenty-three) of Concord lingered at the Lexington home of his fiancée, Lydia Mulliken (age twenty-one), to whom, in the custom of the day, he was paying his address or courting. Being a woman of grace and beauty, she reportedly had many suitors but had chosen the doctor as her betrothed.

The evening air was cool and crisp from a light rain and the blossom smells of early spring were evident. A low, bright, rising moon illuminated the countryside. It was a time of awakening and romance but also of sinister deeds and events. An unusual amount of activity was occurring this night, and what had begun as a nocturnal period for affection would be jolted into a day of anger and war that was to influence the lives of two lovers.

Lydia lived with her widowed mother, four brothers and two sisters in a home across Cambridge Road from Munroe's Tavern (which still exists). Her older sibling, Nathaniel, worked his late father's clock shop and was a member of Captain John Parker's militia company. Prescott, a third-generation doctor with seven siblings, was a handsome, intelligent romantic. Although exempt from military duty due to his profession, he and his brother Abel were staunch supporters of liberty and volunteered as messengers and alarm riders.

Soon after 12:30 a.m. on April 19, Prescott took leave of Lydia, mounted his bay mare and struck out for home, riding past the Lexington Common.

Lydia wistfully watches after her departing fiancé as he rides in the direction of Lexington Common toward his Concord home, unknowing of the historic events about to unfold. *Photograph by Dennis Dostie, MMNHP volunteer.*

Fatefully, he encountered two other travelers—Paul Revere and William Dawes—hastening on their way to warn Concord's officials of approaching British Regulars. The doctor was recognized as a "high son of Liberty" who knew the area and was thus asked to join in the errand.

It was decided that along the route, every inhabitant should be alarmed and Prescott's recognizable presence would give credence to the message. Dawes and the doctor had stopped at a house near the Bull Tavern on the Lincoln-Lexington town line, where Lincoln minuteman Nathaniel Baker was courting his future wife Elizabeth Taylor (records indicate they may have already been married). Revere sped ahead and was approached by two men who tried to force him from the road. Calling up his two companions, he was then cornered by six more members of the British army patrol who were on the road watching for colonial messengers. Meanwhile, Baker quickly took the alarm to central and southern Lincoln.

When Prescott realized the situation, he exclaimed, "Put on!" to his companions, jumped his mare over a low stone wall and raced down a rough farm road that led to the swampy lowlands of a local river. Dawes wheeled about and galloped full speed toward Lexington. Revere was captured.

Prescott (left rear) and Dawes are waylaid by a patrol of British army officers. The doctor escapes over the wall to continue alarming Lincoln and Concord. *Photograph by Dennis Dostie, MMNHP volunteer.*

Prescott, full of excitement and fear, but burning with a purpose, rode his horse out of the swamp cover and arrived at the tavern of Ephraim Hartwell, where he rapped on the door and announced, "The Regulars are coming!" He then proceeded westward along the Bay Road to Concord, his duty in Lincoln accomplished. Hartwell sent his servant girl to warn his son Samuel, a sergeant in the Lincoln minute company, who lived some hundred yards down the road. She managed the task but when she balked out of fear at continuing the errand, Samuel's wife Mary promptly handed her baby to the servant and ran herself to the home of Captain William Smith, commander of the Lincoln minute company, to give him the warning.

Arriving in Concord center near 1:30 a.m., Prescott informed Meeting House guard Amos Melvin of the approaching danger and the alarm bell was rung. Tradition and stories state that the doctor continued his ride to Acton and Stow announcing, "Rouse your men... the British are marching on Lexington and Concord," thus mustering the military forces of those villages.

Meanwhile, Abel Prescott Jr., Samuel's brother, was dispatched to spread the alarm through the towns of Sudbury and Framingham, Massachusetts, farther to the west. He returned to Concord about noon via the town's South Bridge, just as the Regulars were departing. He was sighted and shot by a British soldier. The musket ball lodged in his side and within four months, at age twenty-six, he died of a combination of the wound and dysentery. Thus began a series of tragedies for the Prescott and Mulliken families.

While the retreating British military column fought its way eastward toward Boston, a relief brigade from that town arrived in Lexington and set a defensive formation near Munroe's Tavern. Within its perimeter were the home and clock shop of the Mulliken family, who had by this time fled to a neighbor's house. As the soldiers vacated town, they looted and burned the Mulliken buildings to the ground, acts that unfortunately were repeated again before the day was done. The family later submitted a damage bill to the Provincial Congress for some 431 pounds sterling to cover the lost house, shop, furniture, wearing apparel, clocks and clock tools.

Lydia's brother, Nathaniel, survived the skirmish on the common and the later ambush of the retreating Regulars only to die of camp fever at age twenty-four while with the provincial army at Cambridge. Lydia and her family moved in with a neighbor before obtaining another home in Lexington and though their relationship was strained by the events, her love for Samuel Prescott continued unabated.

Dr. Prescott had already lost an uncle to the Indians in 1744 and now in 1775 a brother to the Regulars. Yet according to one source (*Massachusetts*

Soldiers and Sailors of the American Revolution), he next appeared in service at Fort Ticonderoga in 1776 under the heading "Hartwell Brook the first Everidge" listed as "Dr. 'Sall' Prescot." He was also reported to have gone to sea aboard a privateer, captured by the British navy and imprisoned at Halifax, Nova Scotia. Among family papers of a Jacob Winter (Windrow) of Ashburnham, Massachusetts, was found a letter claiming that he had been a prison mate of a Dr. Prescott from Concord who apparently died in miserable conditions during 1777.

Lydia, the dutiful betrothed, waited some seven years for her love to return. But as time passed, her memories of the doctor dimmed and no word or correspondence arrived. Finally as the Revolution was ending, she abandoned hope of ever seeing Samuel again. Lydia met and married Joseph Burrell on November 25, 1782, moved to Haverhill, Massachusetts, and raised a family. She died on October 21, 1789, at the young age of thirty-six. Prescott's brother Benjamin served as a Continental army surgeon and two of Lydia's brothers also saw military duty during the Revolution.

Thus concluded the saga of two families brought together by the love of their children. They had been intimately involved in historic, heroic events of the day and eventually were shattered by those same events and war. Such were the human aspects of April 19, 1775, personal details that are often lost in the traditional telling of history. Such also were the real lives of lovers Dr. Samuel Prescott of Concord and Lydia Mulliken of Lexington.

NOTE: Artist Thomas Sully (1783–1872) produced three paintings portraying the April 19 story of Samuel and Lydia. Though not historically accurate, they depict the courting, receiving the news of the British Regulars marching and bidding goodbye as he begins his ride. These paintings were once in the Collyer Collection at the Bennington, Vermont Historical Museum and Art Gallery, but now are lost. Photocopies may be seen at the Special Collections, Concord Free Public Library.

Castle, Norman. *The Minute Men 1775–1975*. Southborough, MA: Yankee Colour Corporation, 1977.

Dawes, C. Burr. *William Dawes—First Rider of the Revolution—Chronological Narrative*. OH: Historic Gardens Press, 1976.

Hudson, Charles. *History of the Town of Lexington, Middlesex County, Massachusetts from Its First Settlement to 1868*. 2 vols. Boston: Houghton Mifflin Company, 1913.

MacLean, John C. *A Rich Harvest: The History, Buildings and People of Lincoln, Massachusetts*. Portsmouth, NH: Lincoln Historical Society, Peter E. Randall, publisher, 1987.

Mulliken, Dr. John. "Samuel Prescott: Physician—Patriot." *Archives of Surgery* 110 (April 1975).

Tourtellot, Arthur N. *William Diamond's Drum*. Garden City, NY: Doubleday & Company, 1959.

Viets, H.R. "Samuel Prescott and His Midnight Ride." *New England Journal of Medicine* 254 (1956): 716–61.

James Barrett
A Patriot's Name for Posterity

Soldier. Statesman. Husband. Father. Farmer. Gentleman. Man of God. Concordian. "As great a patriot as was then or perhaps ever was in Concord…his name should be honorably handed down to posterity." These words by Private Thaddeus Blood bear testimony to the man who orchestrated the events surrounding "the shot heard round the world" and who was known to his countrymen as James Barrett.

Born July 29, 1710, in Concord to blacksmith and farmer Benjamin and Lydia (Minott) Barrett, James traced his family to participants in King Philip's War of the 1670s. In marrying Rebecca Hubbard, he became related to Concord's founder and its first minister, Reverend Peter Bulkeley, and he eventually raised a family of five sons and four daughters. He earned a living as both a highly successful miller and farmer (produce and livestock) and early in life became engaged in the military and political arenas for the benefit of his fellow citizens and town.

During the French and Indian War, he fought with distinction as a captain of militia at Oswego, New York (1755–56), under Colonel (later Commander in Chief and Governor) William Shirley of Massachusetts. He also saw action at Fort Ticonderoga, New York (1758), under Major General James Abercromby and at Crown Point, New York (1759), under Major General/Lord Jeffrey Amherst. A person of unusual courage but of solid common sense, Barrett had a distinctive strong physical appearance and was recognized to have a forceful personality and good leadership skills. In December 1757 he and other military leaders unsuccessfully supported the formation of a picket or provincial guard to defend against French and Indian attacks on Massachusetts. Though shunned at the time, this unique concept would be adopted in later years by a Provincial Congress in the form of immediate ready or minute companies for protection against British Regulars in 1774–75.

Barrett had already served the town of Concord politically as a selectman (1754, 1755, 1760) and a representative to the Great and General Court of Massachusetts (1756, 1757, 1764). So following the war with the French and Indians his fellow townsmen selected him again to represent their views on critical issues of the day. In September 1768 Barrett was back sitting in the General Court in Boston. In that same year, his productive farm became a source of food for the king's soldiers (as it had during the recent war) who were now stationed in Boston to quell Townsend Act riots.

Always outspoken, in 1773 Barrett raised concerns about the unconstitutional acts of Parliament and infringement on colonial rights. Thus it was not surprising that his townsmen continually selected him to serve as their representative until the royal governor disbanded the General Court in 1774. Barrett was then chosen by Concord to participate in the emergency Middlesex County Convention, and soon after as a delegate to the new (and illegal) Provincial Congress. For a variety of reasons (most especially political), he stopped supplying food to the British army in 1774.

Be it town meetings or congressional conferences, people were accustomed to looking to the wise, clever, brave, solid Christian Barrett for counsel before embarking upon a course of action. With the probability that the conflict with England would increase in intensity, the Provincial Congress during its October 1774 meetings in Concord reorganized the militia. The intent was to have an Army of Observation for defense in response to incursions into the countryside by the Regulars from Boston. Barrett was asked to accept the rank of colonel commanding a militia regiment, in addition to being superintendent of the military stores being gathered in the Concord depot. Hair gray, legs and knees weak, approaching age sixty-five but still stout of heart, he reluctantly accepted. His fellow townsmen caused his change of mind by stating, "We don't want active service, we only want your advice." This would be altered quickly when the moment of conflict arrived.

On Easter Sunday, April 16, 1775, Concord's military and civilian officials received a warning from Paul Revere that Royal Governor General Thomas Gage had plans to march British Regulars to Concord to destroy their weapons and supplies. It was believed that perhaps an additional objective might be to take Barrett prisoner because of his considerable influence in the

Barrett (second from left) with his wife and daughter encourage local militiamen as they go about hiding military supplies. *Photograph by Dennis Dostie, MMNHP volunteer.*

cause of liberty. While this was not found in Gage's final orders to Lieutenant Colonel Francis Smith, the idea may either have been issued verbally or come to mind when the Regulars reached Barrett's farm. The forewarning led to the hurried relocation and secreting of arms and materials—especially cannon—both within and away from Concord. Meanwhile, Barrett also promulgated strategies for his minute and militia units in anticipation of the expected invasion of his town.

At about 7:30 a.m. on Wednesday, April 19, the inevitable occurred. A seemingly endless column of Regulars (about seven hundred) approached Concord. In the face of these overwhelming odds, Barrett wisely adhered to his plan to defend, not attack. The intention was to hold the militia back and withdraw from harm—even to the detriment of stores—to avoid conflict and let the king's soldiers be the provokers. This allowed time for the provincial forces to increase in numbers. With some two hundred men, mostly from Concord and Lincoln, Barrett marched across North Bridge north along the river to Punkatasset Hill overlooking the bridge. While his force increased in size to eventually

Colonel Barrett's house, circa 1775, as sketched in 1848. *Reprinted from* The Pictorial Field-Book of the Revolution, *2 volumes, by Benson John Lossing, 1850; O'Neill Library, Boston College.*

some four hundred men, he moved closer to the bridge onto a farm field of his second in command, Major John Buttrick. Within the provincial ranks prepared to fight stood one militia company commanded by his son, Captain Nathan Barrett (later wounded chasing the Redcoats to Charlestown), and another commanded by son-in-law Captain George Minot.

The force of Regulars that arrived at the bridge split, and four companies—a total of about 125 men—marched off in the direction of Barrett's farm. Three companies of some 95 men remained to guard the river crossing. Suffering from age, infirmity and sheer excitement and extremely concerned for his family's well being, Barrett galloped home to ensure Rebecca and the children were well and prepare for an unwelcome visitation by the king's soldiers. He then returned to his command. A traditional tale notes that he passed the Regulars on their way to his farm and after the fight at the bridge he passed them again when he returned to check on the welfare of his family. Amazingly he apparently roused little suspicions by the Redcoats and was not stopped in either instance.

Upon seeing smoke rise from town and fearing that it was being destroyed, Barrett reacted to the urgings of his adjutant, Lieutenant Joseph Hosmer, and ordered his forces to march across the North Bridge and into town. Buttrick and Lieutenant Colonel John Robinson of Westford, Massachusetts (on the field with no troops of his own), led the column, with Captain Isaac Davis and his Acton minute company at the column's head. Colonel Barrett rode along the line exhorting his men not to fire first but fire fast if they were attacked. His mature, confident manner eased the fear and anxiety felt by all.

As the provincials approached the bridge, a few Regulars fired warning shots that were followed by a deadly Redcoat volley that killed Davis and one of his private soldiers, Abner Hosmer. Buttrick issued what was believed to be the very first order that day by a provincial officer to fire on the king's soldiers. The ensuing musketry killed and wounded numbers of the enemy, precipitating a disorderly retreat back to Concord center. Westford oral tradition later claimed that Robinson gave the command or shouted it simultaneously with Buttrick.

Barrett moved quickly to regain control of his dissolving companies. After a short respite, he gave orders to keep the older militia men (alarm companies) to the rear and on the west side of the bridge, while many of the minutemen and militia took cover on an easterly hill behind a wall under Buttrick's command. Barrett had the provincial dead removed to Buttrick's nearby house and the wounded taken to his house for care. At this point, the colonel seems to have removed himself from the field for the day. Returning home, he met his regimental lieutenant colonel, Ezekiel How(e), whose companies from Framingham and Sudbury had already been diverted eastward toward the Meriam's Corner/Brooks Hill area by Barrett's son Stephen. Nothing more appears regarding the activities of the aged Colonel Barrett on April 19.

Barrett was uneasy about the process and plans to lay siege to Boston, and he urged that the Continental Congress should quickly appoint a commander in chief over all military forces for the conflict ahead. And so it did, finally selecting for the unenviable task a Virginian with military experience—George Washington. His Excellency arrived at Cambridge on July 2 following the June 17 Breed's (Bunker's) Hill battle. Not until the evacuation on March 17, 1776, was Boston cleared of the king's soldiers and their supporters.

His military command and fighting days over, Barrett remained involved for many years in the political aspects of the war for independence. In October of 1776 along with his son James, Esquire, he sat on a town committee that debated whether the House of Representatives and Council should enact a constitution or form a government for the state. Barrett argued against the House drafting a constitution, and requested instead that a representative body of the citizens—not legislators—prepare the crucial document. In addition, he sought to ensure a fair distribution of powers between the executive, legislative and judicial sectors. When the drafted constitution from the General Court was rejected in Concord in June 1778, a state Constitutional Convention was convened in 1779 and its document concerning the organization of the state finally passed a Concord vote in May 1780, with some changes. Barrett's sage advice was still sought and followed.

In his declining years, Barrett remained in service to Concord and the revolutionary cause, including membership on the Committees of Correspondence and Inspection. In conjunction with the Board of War, he was appointed an agent responsible for gathering and delivering shoes, shirts and socks to the North and South departments of the Continental army.

Barrett lived to see the Declaration of Independence, but not the successful conclusion of the war and the formation of a United States of America. He died suddenly at home on April 11, 1779. A well-attended, solemn funeral took place at the Hill Burying Ground in Concord and the epitaph on his stone containing the family coat of arms read, "courteous, benevolent, charitable…fidelity, uprightness, esteemed…warm attachment to…careful practice of religion…worthy character…just." What more could be said of the man who served his town in war and peace and was instrumental in taking decisive actions at the very moment of truth in which the movement toward a nation's independence began?

NOTE: Barrett's historic house has been owned by only two families since its construction in 1705—the Barrett family, 1705–1904, and the McGrath family, 1904–2004. It is presently under the care and ownership of the nonprofit preservation organization "Save Our Heritage," which has the goal of stabilizing, restoring and preserving the structure in anticipation of having it accepted by Congress as part of Minute Man National Historic Park, Concord.

Fenn, Mary R. *Old Houses of Concord*. Concord: Old Concord Chapter DAR, 1974.

Fischer, David Hackett. *Paul Revere's Ride*. New York: Oxford University Press, 1994.

Galvin, General John R. *The Minute Men*. McLean, VA: Pergamon-Brassey's International Defense Publishers, 1989.

Greeley, Dana McLean. *Know These Concordians*. Concord: First Parish Church Publications Office, 1975.

Ripley, Reverend Ezra. *A History of the Fight at Concord, on the 19th of April, 1775*. Concord: Allen & Atwill, 1827.

Shattuck, Lemuel. *History of the Town of Concord to 1832*. Boston: Russell, Odiorne, and Company, 1835.

Wheeler, Ruth R. *Concord: Climate for Freedom*. Yarmouthport, MA: Printing and Publishing Production Associates, 1967.

Espionage, Spies and Intrigue Surround Concord

"Know thy enemy" is an ancient military axiom, and by early 1775 the Boston Rebels under Dr. Joseph Warren had an elaborate spy network to monitor British military plans. Some people even believe that Royal Governor General Thomas Gage's colonial-born wife, Margaret Kemble Gage, aided her countrymen, though no factual proof of that exists. Not to be outdone, the governor instituted his own espionage system and established Concord as a primary target.

Gage and his Chief Intelligence Officer (and brother-in-law) Major Stephen Kemble obtained the services of Dr. Benjamin Church, a member of the Provincial Congress and Committee of Safety. The doctor had an expensive mistress and spying brought ready cash. Thus, while Congress met in Concord (October 11–14, 1774; March 22–April 15, 1775), Church, sworn to secrecy, regularly provided summaries of the proceedings to Gage.

Once Concord had become a military center and storehouse for supplies and weapons, it also became a target for espionage. On March 20, Gage sent Captain John Brown and Ensign Henry De Berniere to town disguised in the brown clothes and red handkerchiefs of "Yankee rustics." They were ordered "to reconnoitre and find out the state of the provincial magazines; what number of cannon, etc. they have and in what condition." Roads and terrain were to be noted and sketched.

At Concord, the spies asked directions to Tory Daniel Bliss's house from a woman who accommodated them and later received threats to her welfare. Bliss, whose sister married Patriot minister Reverend William Emerson,

Dr. Benjamin Church, following a just-recessed Provincial Congress meeting, awaits a nocturnal visit by an agent from Gage in order to pass along "secrets." *Photograph by Dennis Dostie, MMNHP volunteer.*

unabashedly hosted the visitors to dinner and provided detailed information on all supplies and weapons and where they could be found. Receiving threats to his own life, he accepted the spies' escort to the safety of Boston, never to return home. Reverend Emerson later remarked, "Verily our enemies are of our own households." De Berniere's report to Gage noted fourteen cannon; two mortars; magazine of powder, cartridges and lead; and stores of flour, fish, salt and rice. It also detailed roads, houses, a river and two bridges, features drawn on a map that would find good use on April 19.

Among Gage's spy papers were two intriguing letters written in poor French by a person who apparently lived in or near Concord and obviously had an intimate knowledge of the town, its people and provincial affairs. Dated March 9 and 11, the messages detailed buildings and the location of weapons and materials including "a large amount of munitions," four brass cannon, ten iron cannon (at the Town House), two mortars, small arms and various supplies. Storage sites included the homes of James Barrett, Ebenezer Hubbard, Samuel Jones and Samuel Whitney. (The Barrett and Whitney structures still exist.) A concluding statement referred to the Reverend Emerson as "nomme Emmerson, un tres mauvais sujet" or a "very bad subject" of the king.

Other unknown agents provided reports to Gage on the sessions of Congress in Concord. Examples included: March 30—an alarm system and criteria for assembling the militia, articles of war and regulations for a constitutional army, need for secrecy; April 3—response to the March 30 movement of British troops in and out of Boston, plans to act on any hostile movement and oppose such movement; April 9—raising of an army of observation, decision to do so before British troops begin movements; April 15—plans for a New England army of eighteen thousand men (eight thousand from Massachusetts).

One informer noted that cannon and munitions boxes were hidden in the woods between "the River and Malden Pond" (Walden Pond). A mysterious "John Hall" (a Concord farmer or a merchant?) reported on deserters escaping Boston and on items (including cannon) hidden at Barrett's farm. Though few in numbers, Concord Tories often passed information to Gage. Captain Jonas Minot, for example, informed his Boston Loyalist friends of being pressured to prepare his company to oppose the Regulars. Provincial response plans made at the time of the "Charlestown powder incident" (September 1774; Redcoats removed powder from a colonial powder house, claiming it belonged to the king) were relayed to the governor's office. Merchant and former slave trader Duncan Ingraham, a man holding Loyalist sentiments, hosted British officers for dinner at his house and was thought to often discuss "sensitive information."

A most controversial, intriguing and very suspect spy was "John Howe." He was said to have dressed as a countryman and allegedly visited Concord on April 11 by order of Gage. Howe entered Concord under the pretense of being a Maine gunsmith willing to assist the Patriot cause. He supposedly was introduced to Major John Buttrick and was shown military storage sites before departing town to retrieve his gunsmith equipment. Instead he quickly reported to Gage.

In various writings, Howe the spy has been listed as a civilian, an officer, a sergeant and a batman/servant (supposedly to spy Captain Brown). However, there exist no 1775 Boston resources—civilian or military—that provide name recognition or support any of these claims. There was a newspaper publisher named John Howe at the time in Boston but a close examination deflects any thought that he was the infamous spy. Dr. David Hackett Fischer in *Paul Revere's Ride* does list a Lieutenant John Howe with the Thirty-eighth Regiment's grenadier company. However, period British military expert Vincent J-R Kehoe has a Lieutenant George Hamilton posted in the same unit position. A final obscure mention of Howe has him as a corporal in the Fifty-second Regiment but no military record has this confirmed.

The amazing Howe saga details his escape from Concord with the help of a Lincoln, Massachusetts "Tory Gore" (possibly John, with Loyalist family connections), followed by an April 12 meeting with Gage. The spy reportedly spoke against an expedition to Worcester by Regulars, but favored instead a foray to Concord using a mounted force of five hundred men. Nothing in the expansive Gage manuscript collection and papers at the William Clements Library, University of Michigan, has yet provided credence to any of these statements.

Of particular note is the fact that when the De Berniere spy papers and reports related to the April 19 Concord expedition are placed side by side with the Howe story and journal, great similarities are found. This is in addition to the difficult-to-comprehend tales of heroics of this single person on April 19, during the Revolution and even in the War of 1812. It should also be of interest that when the British military forces and royal sympathizers evacuated Boston on March 17, 1776, De Berniere's spy papers and reports were inadvertently left behind undisturbed. John Gill, Court Street publisher and co-owner of *The Boston Gazette and Country Journal*, printed the entire text in 1779 under the title "Gen. Gage's Instructions...Account of the Transactions of the British Troops."

A "journal" attributed to Howe surfaced in New Hampshire documenting his amazing spy story, other tales of April 1775 and his life into the nineteenth century. Published in 1827 by a Luther Roby, it appeared under the title *The Journal Kept by Mr. John Howe while He Was Employed as a British Spy*. Unfortunately it was accepted then, and to some degree now, as the truth. Numerous questions persist as to who this man Howe was, and why none of his individual tales have been substantiated by anyone else, including Gage, and whether he even existed. While many unsuspecting historians into the twenty-first century have assumed authenticity, too many doubts persist. The printed journals of 1827 are more likely than not embellished "plagiarism" (a legal concept not accepted or enforced at the time) from De Berniere's spy reports and papers and thus a hoax possibly perpetrated to raise money.

Gage did have two final authentic documents to help him make his fateful April decision related to Concord. A letter explained, "Last Saturday the 7th [actually 8th] of April P:____ R:____ toward evening arrived in Concord, carrying a letter that was to be from Mr. W[arre]n." Revere rode to warn town leaders that an attack was imminent but that the date was still unknown. He made a similar visit to Hancock and Adams in Lexington on April 16. On April 18, Gage received another message, most likely written in Boston, that stated while military stores were being moved from Concord, the town still contained large amounts of provisions and several cannon. Perhaps of special interest to the governor were comments that suggested the two brass cannon stolen from Boston by provincials might be among those in Concord, and that numerous materials were located westward across the North Bridge at Colonel James Barrett's farm.

Gage's reports also explained that Congress had adjourned until May and without its approval and that of surrounding colonies, a provincial army could not be placed in the field. Still more supplies were being received regularly into Massachusetts from Rhode Island and Connecticut. As Congress recessed, it took a parting shot at Parliament that was supposedly seen as a personal affront by Governor Gage, avowing each colony's right to tax and govern itself.

This intelligence, coupled with mounting pressure by Parliament, and especially from Lord Dartmouth, William Legge, secretary of state for America, to act immediately against the Rebels, forced Gage to a decision. He drafted orders for Lieutenant Colonel Francis Smith requiring an expedition to proceed quickly and quietly to destroy all stores and equipment that might be found in Concord. Even late word that sorely needed additional troops were on the way from England could not persuade Gage to wait any longer.

With detailed spy reports and De Berniere as a guide, the search-and-destroy mission went forward. However, due to the expertise of the provincial espionage network, most military items were removed from Concord before Smith's force arrived. Additionally, the alarm had been spread that mobilized thousands of provincial militia and minutemen to observe the Regulars' movements and defend people and property from harm. A volatile scenario was thus created that just might explode into open warfare if a misstep were to occur.

Regarding the spies—British and provincial—in and around Boston in 1774 and 1775, most of them entered history unknown and unnoticed. General George Washington, however, uncovered Dr. Church through the physician's mistress and a captured spy note in cipher. His Excellency publicized the treachery and had the doctor removed from his post as surgeon general of the Continental army. Washington wanted him hanged for treason but no law existed at the time to provide for such action. Dishonored and imprisoned in Connecticut, Church eventually died in a shipwreck on the way to exile. "John Howe" continues to be an enigma. There is still no documentation yet found in Gage's manuscripts, British military records or colonial papers to solidify his existence. Neither are there records to identify the mysterious Concord "Frenchman." Daniel Bliss, Esquire, removed himself and his family from Boston to Canada and eventually became a judge and a gentleman of note in New Brunswick.

Concord returned to being a quiet farming community and struggled to survive the impact of war. At one point the town vied unsuccessfully to become the capital of Massachusetts, or at least its judicial center. But for several months in early 1775, it was the focal point for major intrigue, espionage and intelligence gathering by provincials and British military alike. What was discovered and shared led to the momentous events of April 19 and the beginnings of a revolution.

NOTE: We do not know the true identity of the mysterious British army officer "Captain Brown" who traveled on spy missions to Worcester and Concord with Ensign De Berniere. In some sources he is listed simply as Brown and in others as John Brown. At least one reference is made to him as William Browne of the Fifty-second Regiment.

Bakeless, John. *Turncoats, Traitors & Heroes*. New York: Da Capo Press, 1959.

Courtney, W.B. "Getting to the Bottom of U.S. History." *Boston Herald*, magazine section, March 28, 1928.

French, Allen. *Gen. Gage's Informers*. Ann Arbor: University of Michigan Press, 1932.

Gross, Robert A. *The Minutemen and Their World*. New York: Hill and Wang, 1976.

Kehoe, Colonel Vincent J-R. *We Were There*. Chelmsford, MA: issued by the author, two parts, 1974, 1975.

Roby, Luther. *The Journal Kept by Mr. John Howe While He Was Employed as a British Spy*. Limited issue by author, an original in the Massachusetts Historical Society, 1827.

Travis, Harold G. "The Spy That Hid in Weston." *Weston Historical Society Bulletin* 11, no. 3 (Weston, MA, March 1975).

Williams, Daniel E. "Specious Spy: The Narrative Lives—and Lies—of Mr. John Howe." *Eighteenth Century Theory and Interpretation* 34, no. 3 (Lubbock: Texas Tech. University Press, 1993): 264–86.

A Place of Honor
Charles Miles in Extraordinary Times

Concord, January 17th 1775...then we chose our officers and settled the Company of Minute Men under the command of Cap Charls Miles." So recorded David Hartwell, orderly sergeant for the Concord company, as he would do until the unit disbanded on May 6, 1775. It then amalgamated into the new Massachusetts militia company of Concord's Captain Abishai Brown at Cambridge. But with this January election began life's zenith for Charles Miles, third generation of a Concord founding family, and an under-appreciated figure in the events of April 19, 1775.

John Miles, declared a freeman at Concord in 1639, had by 1663 acquired over four hundred acres of land in the town's South Quarter (Nine Acre Corner area). His son Samuel constructed a house on "faier haven way" (present Williams Road) in the early 1700s, where his son Charles would be born on June 28, 1727, and live most of his life. Religious controversy surrounded the family in 1745 when Deacon Samuel Miles and nineteen other men left First Parish in a dispute over theology with Reverend Daniel Bliss. They formed the West or Black Horse Church in a schism that had social implications for many years.

Like his father, Charles farmed (one hundred acres), gained a solid reputation and became active in town affairs. In addition to working on highways and bridges, in 1754 he was elected a hogreeve, responsible to oversee hogs, pigs and swine—their movements about town and any damage disputes.

Due to Concord's religious upheaval, Charles's first marriage to Zeruiah on November 18, 1756, was outside the church and conducted by Justice of the Peace Thomas Whiting, Esquire. After giving birth to Charles Jr. in June 1757, Zeruiah died of complications in July. Having received church reconciliation, Miles's next marriage to Ruth Barrett on May 3, 1759, was performed by the Reverend Daniel Bliss. Charles's service to the community continued in such positions as surveyor and constable before he took an active role in establishing a regular school (#3) in the Nine Acre Corner district.

By 1771, Miles was prominent enough to be commissioned a militia lieutenant. When Concord organized its first minute company on January 17, 1775, its volunteers consisted mainly of men from the South Quarter who selected one of their own to command—Charles Miles. Each volunteer—Miles, nine officers, a fifer, a drummer and forty-two men—took an oath to defend His Majesty King George the Third his person, crown and dignity; to defend all and every of their charter rights, liberties and privileges; to be ready on a minute's warning to respond with arms and ammunition; and at all times and in all places to obey orders of the men chosen as their officers and of all superior officers.

The new captain went about his business seriously, requesting that the town supply muskets for those in need, provide for a drum and establish disciplinary measures, including fines for men delinquent in their duties. His company had its first drill on January 20, and then met for a half day twice per week thereafter, with each man paid by the town for this training. Prior to the historic fight on April 19, 1775, Miles's minutemen mustered some twenty times with Sergeant Hartwell making accounts of everyone not in attendance.

When word of the approaching king's soldiers was received in Concord, Miles mustered his company on the town common near the Wright Tavern. Included with the unit muster roll that day was a handwritten note by Sergeant Hartwell stating, "Concord, April 19th 1775, then the battel begune."

Later, on the high ground above North Bridge where the colonial force reformed after abandoning Concord center, Miles joined an officers' conference. Possible courses of action were discussed. Upon seeing columns of smoke rising from town, it was decided that the provincial force would march into town in order to stop the destruction. The opportunity and honor to lead the minute and militia units to the bridge, past the defending Regulars, was supposedly offered to a Concord captain who reportedly said he "should rather not go." As Miles commanded the senior minute company (Captain David Brown commanded the town's second minute company),

Miles addresses members of his minute company following a March 13, 1775 muster and drill. *Photograph by Dennis Dostie, MMNHP volunteer.*

speculation was that he might have uttered the reply. No factual sources have substantiated this incident. It should be noted, however, that Captain Isaac Davis, commander of the Acton minute company, was asked if he was afraid to go. His response was that he was not afraid and neither were his men.

History notes that Davis and his company led the march to the bridge and while the position of other units is uncertain, several accounts place Miles's company second (or third) in line. For certain, they were in the thick of this historic engagement. Whether from a sense of duty, emotion or regret at not having taken the lead in the march, Miles later led his townsmen in chasing the Regulars back to Charlestown. During the fighting, though initially incorrectly listed as killed, he did receive a wound in one hand caused by an enemy musket ball.

In succeeding weeks, Miles's company responded to alarms in Concord and Cambridge, with the final orderly book entries noting that guard duty was stood for twenty-four hours on May 5 and 6. His son Charles Jr. (later a militia captain himself) served as a private in a Concord company at Roxbury in March 1776 during the Boston siege and the town's eventual evacuation by the Crown forces. Although his minute company dissolved and members joined new militia units, during June 1776 Miles raised another company himself that included sixty-one Concord men. This unit joined a five-thousand-man force that marched 250 miles to reinforce Fort Ticonderoga, which was under a British army attack. Concord's Reverend William Emerson participated in this expedition as a chaplain to the American army and died of camp fever in October. Upon returning home, Miles would again be called to duty at Boston (1777) and Cambridge (1778).

Years later, Reverend Ezra Ripley noted that upon being asked his feelings when marching to the bridge on April 19, Miles responded that "he went to the service of the day with the same seriousness and acknowledgement of God which he carried to church."

Post–Revolution years were difficult for Miles, and a 1781 shoemaker's receipt book listed him as a butcher. Apparently business experimentations and gambling led to great indebtedness. On November 2, 1790, at age sixty-three, Miles passed away due to "heredity delerium," according to Reverend Ripley.

A "Charles Miles" continued residing in the family house (which still stands at 429 Williams Road) until grandson Charles (known to Henry David Thoreau) moved to Fitchburg around 1858 and the building was sold at auction. Maps through the 1860s carried the notations "C. Miles," "Miles Swamp" (off Marlboro Road), "C. Miles Run" and "Miles Mill." Thoreau wrote in 1852 of the lavish flora abounding at "Miles Blueberry Swamp."

But the legacy of Charles Miles would be that he lived in an extraordinary time (social, political, religious and military) in Concord history, was elected captain of his town's first minute company, led his men against the king's soldiers at North Bridge and was one of only four Concord men wounded on April 19. For these reasons alone, Captain Charles Miles deserves a place of honor among the renowned names in the storied past of Concord Town.

Gross, Robert A. *The Minutemen and Their World*. New York: Hill and Wang, 1976.

Miles, Jonas M. *Miles Genealogy*. Boston: C.E. Goodspeed & Company, 1920.

Ripley, Reverend Ezra. *A History of the Fight at Concord, on the 19th of April, 1775*. Concord: Allen & Atwill, 1827.

Shattuck, Lemuel. *History of the Town of Concord to 1832*. Boston: Russell, Odiorne, and Company, 1835.

Survey of Historical and Architectural Resources, Concord, MA 3. Concord Historical Commission, 1994.

Tolman, George. *The Concord Minute Men*. Read before the Concord Antiquarian Society, March 4, 1901. Chelmsford, MA: Society for the Preservation of Colonial Culture, 1968.

Weisfeld, Janice. *The Miles Family in Colonial Concord*. 1975.

Whatever Can Go Wrong Will Go Wrong

An old adage oft called Murphy's Law reads, "Whatever can go wrong will go wrong." This proverb might aptly be applied to the events of April 19, 1775, when challenges and difficulties plagued both the colonists and the British army expedition to Concord.

To counter and defensively react to any movement of British Regulars out of Boston, the well-meaning Massachusetts Provincial Congress established volunteer immediate response units called minute companies that came from the towns' militia units.

It should be explained that, under provincial law, all males age sixteen to sixty (with limited exceptions to include Negroes, ministers, doctors and Harvard College students) were required to serve in their hometown's militia for defense purposes. This was a part of citizenship. These units could occasionally be called to duty for activities beyond their town boundaries. In 1774–75, volunteers from the militia were drawn for the minute companies; units ready to act in emergencies at a moment's notice. Unlike their militia brothers, the minutemen (generally the young, energetic and agile) drilled weekly, elected their officers, could be called away from home for at least a day, were well equipped and were paid for drill and service. Men exempt from service, usually due to age, infirmity or because they were otherwise unable to meet militia requirements, could be placed in an alarm company (1775) for extraordinary situations requiring home defense only.

Once the Provincial Congress had established minute companies to augment the regular militia, it then organized all of the companies into regiments, each with their own command structures. In the Concord area of Middlesex County alone, there existed a minute regiment of eight companies and a militia regiment of seven companies. While reasonable on paper, the concept went awry in the field amidst the turmoil of the descent of the Regulars upon Concord on April 19.

As the senior officer present in Concord on April 19, 1775, Colonel James Barrett (militia) inherited a disjointed force of minute, militia and alarm companies along with unit officers and staff. He appointed Major John Buttrick (minute) his field commander, who in turn chose a reluctant Lieutenant Joseph Hosmer (horse troop) to be his adjutant. These Concord men were responsible for organizing into a cohesive military force, a rapidly growing group of some ten mixed companies as well as unattached individuals such as Lieutenant Colonel John Robinson of Westford, Massachusetts (of Colonel James Prescott's militia regiment), who had few of his men present.

Scrambling to retreat from Concord center in the face of overwhelming odds, and to reform atop Punkatasset Hill above North Bridge to await reinforcements, Barrett's army was joined by women, children, civilians and dogs—some fleeing the Regulars and some just curious. In the chaos of a dangerous military situation, the officers of necessity spent time ushering the non-combatants to a safe location. Eventually the provincial force moved to a farm field that was close to Major Buttrick's house and afforded a better view of the bridge.

In the midst of this confusion, a Lincoln man, James Nichols, who had recently arrived in the colony, was of age and thus serving in the militia, reportedly said, "I will go down and talk with them [Regulars at the Bridge]." Passing his firelock to another man, he went forward and apparently had words with soldiers of the Tenth Regiment Light Infantry company. Returning after a short time, he gathered his musket and went home, unsure if he wished to participate in any upcoming possibilities. The day's first deserter must have caused questions of resolve to filter through the ranks.

A council involving officers, selectmen and members of the Committee of Correspondence/Vigilance was convened, meaning that military decisions would be made through a consensus involving non-professionals and civilians, many with little or no military experience. Possibly in the subconscious of those making judgments lingered historic issues that had already split Concord, including slavery, class distinction, military experience, politics, neighborhood animosity and religious conflict. In a crisis, this was not the ideal situation for a commander.

When the moment "to march into the middle of the town for its defense" arrived, uncertainty arose as to who would lead the force of nearly four hundred men. Allegedly a Concord captain declined the honor. Lincoln's Captain William Smith volunteered but was overlooked, perhaps due to inexperience and/or poorly equipped men. Captain Isaac Davis, commanding a well-trained and outfitted Acton minute company, stepped forward, and when asked if he was afraid to go he noted that he was not, and neither were his men. Davis and Acton thus marched into history.

After the bridge was taken and secured, the provincials should have reorganized and prepared for a counterattack. Instead, command and control seemed to disappear, perhaps in part due to Davis's death and the shock of firing upon and killing the king's soldiers. Some two hundred men joined Major Buttrick in a march to Meriam's Corner to await the retreat of the Regulars from Concord. Other men carried the dead and wounded to nearby houses, while others went off for victuals, and a few individuals just went home. Thaddeus Blood would later recall, "Every one appeared to be his own commander."

In the aftermath of the bridge skirmish, in the heat of the moment perhaps, a young minuteman struck a wounded British soldier on the head with an axe. Regulars returning from the search for military supplies and weapons at Barrett's farm went unchallenged past the disorganized, dispersing colonials. As they rushed from the scene, they observed their comrade's wretched state and reported that the Rebels were scalping and maiming the dead and wounded. This caused fear and anger in the British ranks that later would lead to reprisals.

Sure enough, at nearly 4:40 p.m. when the Redcoats entered the village of Menotomy (today Arlington), frustration, the axe incident, mounting casualties and the unorthodox fighting methods of the provincials took their toll and led to misconduct. Officers were unable to maintain complete control over the emotions and actions of all of their men. Additionally, lack of organization and attention by the provincials to the possibility that they might be surrounded by flanking units from the British army column, coupled with bravado and a false sense of security, set the scenario for a disaster. Almost half of the total casualties for both sides (twenty-eight colonials killed, ten wounded; forty Regulars killed, eighty wounded) occurred in the savage fighting that took place in less than ninety minutes over some two miles of the Bay Road.

Along the retreat route at Jason Russell's Menotomy house (extant), the fifty-eight-year-old owner had stated that "an Englishman's house is his castle" and he decided to remain and protect his property and rights. This

Russell dies at his doorstep at the hands of Redcoat flankers. *Reprinted from* The Fight at the Jason Russell House *by Ruth L. Berry, 1975. Photograph courtesy of the Arlington Historical Society, Arlington, Massachusetts.*

regrettable error in judgment led Russell and eleven other provincials to be slaughtered by Redcoat flankers and soldiers from the column, outside and within the house. Russell himself was shot twice and bayoneted eleven times in his doorway. Two Regulars lost their lives at this place, the bloodiest encounter of the day. An hour or so later, the day's momentous activities would end.

Lieutenant Colonel Francis Smith's plans to quickly and secretly march a force of some seven hundred Regulars from Boston to Concord to destroy or remove military stores and weapons and return safely was also not immune to Murphy's Law. As with Barrett's force, the Smith expedition was an unusual mixture of units (light infantry and grenadiers from each regiment and the marine battalion in Boston), some serving under officers unfamiliar to their troops and few of whom had experienced combat in the last fifteen years. This would lead to a fracturing of discipline and command, and some inability to perform maneuvers properly both at Lexington Common and North Bridge.

Late on the night of April 18, Smith's problems began. A shortage of boats, delays awaiting provisions and a high tide caused the expeditions crossing the Charles River from Boston Common to Cambridge to be hours late. The men were wet and tired as they departed for Concord. Timing and surprise factors were eliminated first when a mounted British patrol allowed the escape of an alarm rider (Dr. Samuel Prescott) who went on to warn Lincoln and Concord. So too again, when Major John Pitcairn (Smith's second in command), leading an advanced force with orders to immediately move with all speed to secure the two Concord bridges, disobeyed those instructions. Whether due to ego or anger, Pitcairn elected to stop and disarm a small militia company standing well off the road on Lexington Common, representing no obstacle to the Regulars. At the common (depending on whose story is believed), someone on one side or the other fired a shot or shots. The Regulars fired a volley and some broke ranks to give chase to the fleeing colonials. The resulting unplanned skirmish resulted in eight dead and ten wounded provincials. King's forces casualties were a sergeant slightly wounded and a horse grazed by a musket ball.

In Concord, instead of just physically destroying some discovered martial stores, British soldiers piled many wooden items and set them afire. The sparks touched off a blaze on the Town House roof. Elderly widow Martha Moulton berated the officers and warned that the building and others in town would be destroyed if the fire were allowed to continue. When no action took place, she grabbed a bucket of water herself, and at that point soldiers were ordered to douse the flames. Contrary to a popular myth, no evidence indicates that there was any gunpowder stored in the Town House attic that would have exploded. However, water tossed on the fire caused unusually heavy black smoke to rise above the town, which led the colonials standing above North Bridge to believe that their village was being destroyed. This resulted in the decision of the "country people" to march in defense of their homes and families. Had the fire and smoke not occurred, would a confrontation at North Bridge and the bloody retreat to Boston have taken place?

Captain Walter S. Laurie, Forty-third Light Infantry, commanding the Regulars guarding the bridge watched the provincial column move toward him. Nervously searching in the direction of the village for the earlier summoned reinforcements (that would arrive too late), he prepared to make a defense. The plan was to employ "street firing," a common technique used to defend narrow thoroughfares that was simple enough to execute if the troops were properly trained. A unit would have the front rank kneel and two stand, fire a volley and peel off to the left

Regulars attempt to defend North Bridge using "street firing" tactics while provincials approach. *Photograph by Dennis Dostie, MMNHP volunteer.*

and right, moving to the rear of the formation to reload, while the next group stepped forward to accomplish the same task. A street or bridge attempting to be used by an opposing force could easily be held as long as ammunition was available.

However, due to lack of experience, discipline and drill, exacerbated by unfamiliar officers being in command, the maneuver failed. Before Laurie had fully arranged his companies, Lieutenant William Sutherland, Thirty-eighth Regiment of Foot, a volunteer and in command of no particular unit, attempted to move soldiers of the Forty-third Regiment into fields on either side of the bridge. Few followed his instructions. It is believed that these men were the first to fire on the colonials without orders, which then led to an imperfect volley from the first ranks of the Fourth Regiment standing at the bridge. A damaging fire from the provincials, breakdown in discipline and communications and a misunderstanding of troop movements occurred, which caused Laurie's force to begin a hasty retreat, abandoning the bridge and their companions still at Barrett's farm. By 1776, Laurie would leave the army and return home to Scotland.

While the scenario at the bridge was occurring, Captain Lawrence Parsons, Tenth Regiment Light Infantry, was leading his four companies—about 125 men—back from Barrett's farm to Concord center. Mrs. Barrett had refused spirits to the Regulars, but along the way, the widow Brown's tavern was encountered and a brief stop was made for refreshment. A young man working at the tavern later recalled hearing shots fired from the direction of the bridge, but as the soldiers did not react, he thought they had not heard them.

Some minutes later, Parsons continued his march and arrived at the bridge only to witness the aftermath of the skirmish. Had he not stopped, most likely his column would have arrived on the scene at North Bridge while the colonials' formation was stretched down the hillside to the bridge. Parsons would have had the opportunity to form line and surprise the provincials with either a shocking musket volley, a bayonet attack or both. How might such have impacted the Concord fight, the day's events and history?

Finally, Brigadier Lord Hugh Percy's relief brigade from Boston was planned to depart on April 19 at 4:00 a.m. but did not muster until 7:00 a.m. and then march at 9:00 a.m. Written orders to the brigade major were secretly delivered and left unopened and unread while the officer slept. The marines mustered late because sealed, delivered orders were unopened by their commander, Major Pitcairn, who was away with Lieutenant Colonel Smith in Concord. These delays most likely led to increased casualties among Smith's expedition and its near annihilation.

The rendering of historical events tends to dwell on the heroic, romantic and positive aspects, and often ignores facts, reality and problems. Yet when real people are involved, it is most likely that a part of the actual equation, even in victory, will be "whatever can go wrong will go wrong." Such was the case on April 19, 1775, when two simple plans, one by the British Regulars and the other by the provincials, interacted with Murphy's Law and changed the course of history.

Coburn, Frank Warren. *The Battle of April 19, 1775*. Boston: Wright & Potter Printing Company, 1922.

Fischer, David Hackett. *Paul Revere's Ride*. New York: Oxford University Press, 1994.

French, Allen. *The Day of Concord and Lexington*. Boston: Little, Brown and Company, 1925.

Gross, Robert A. *The Minutemen and Their World*. New York: Hill and Wang, 1976.

Kehoe, Colonel Vincent J-R. *The British Story of the Battle of Lexington and Concord on the Nineteenth of April 1775*. Los Angeles: Hale & Company MM, 2000.

———. *We Were There*. Chelmsford, MA: issued by the author, two parts, 1974, 1975.

Ripley, Reverend Ezra. *A History of the Fight at Concord, on the 19th of April, 1775*. Concord: Allen & Atwill, 1827.

Smith, Samuel A. *West Cambridge 1775*. Somerville, MA: Fleming & Son, 1974.

An Unfurled Flag and the Concord Fight

"Their flag to April's breeze unfurled..."

To what flag did Emerson allude in his 1836 "Concord Hymn"? Was any flag—British or colonial—displayed in Concord on April 19, 1775, or was the famed author using but poetic license or an allegory to add a detail to his story? There seems to be no evidence of awareness by Emerson that any flag was displayed at North Bridge. Neither does there exist solid factual documentation to support the concept that such a display occurred.

While the presence of at least one flag was documented, its exact design is seemingly lost or questioned at best. As British Regulars entered Concord, Lieutenant John Barker of the Fourth "The King's Own" Regiment noted "taking possession of a hill with a liberty pole on it and a flag flying." Historian Lemuel Shattuck wrote, "Here in the rear of Reuben Brown's stood the pole on which the flag of liberty was first unfurled."

Other accounts verify the pole and its flag standing on a burial hill across from the meetinghouse, but none describe the defiant banner itself. Speculation ranges from the New England pine tree flag; to a red banner with a white canton containing a pine tree; to a blue flag with the Cross of St. George and a pine tree, both in a white canton; to an all white banner with a green liberty tree. In Boston, the Sons of Liberty had posted a liberty pole and hoisted to its top an all red banner. The Honorable John Keyes in Duane Hamilton Hurd's 1890 *History of Middlesex County, Mass.* and Josephine Swayne's *The Story of Concord* (1939) state that the pine tree flag, which represented freedom, flew from the Concord pole. According to the July 16,

Pine-Tree Flag.

Possibly the "people's" or "liberty flag" that was atop the pole in Concord center when the Regulars arrived. *Reprinted from* History of Middlesex County, Massachusetts *by Samuel Adams Drake, Volume I, 1880.*

1888 *Boston Transcript*, the Emerson family tradition holds that "an English banner with 'Union and Liberty' inscribed in white letters" graced the pole. Whatever the design, the flag's symbol of defiance was not lost on the king's soldiers, since they destroyed both it and the pole.

Both in writings and especially in pictorial images, some individuals have reflected a belief that Lieutenant Colonel Francis Smith's military expedition from Boston carried the king's and/or possibly regimental colors into Concord. Regulation and precedent generally governed the use of such standards. Carried by soldiers in the grade of ensign, the flags accompanied troops into battle for such purposes as identifying the unit, boosting morale, serving as a rallying point and helping to align attacking forces. Several ensigns, including Jeremy Lister of the Tenth Regiment (who was wounded at Meriam's Corner) and Henry De Berniere of a battalion company (spy and route guide to Concord and Barrett's farm), were with Smith's column. Neither of them was mentioned in connection with a flag on April 19, nor was Ensign Henry Baldwin in Lord Hugh Percy's relief brigade.

While numerous accounts and narratives of the day's events from both sides describe the Regulars' uniforms, music, swords and bayonets that "glistened in the sun," no flags were alluded to or noted. Smith's force (about seven hundred men) consisted of the elite light infantry and grenadier companies from each of nine regiments and the marine battalion in Boston plus a grenadier company of the Eighteenth Regiment. These units were combined to facilitate effective rapid movement in the accomplishment of a search-and-destroy mission, not necessarily for an open field battle. Since no entire, single regiment participated and surprise, rather than ceremony, was a goal, flags of any type, as prescribed by the British army 1768 Warrant, would not have been carried. This, coupled with a complete lack of any evidence regarding British colors being carried from Boston or entering Concord on April 19, led to the belief that neither occurred.

There has apparently existed through the years in Sudbury, Massachusetts, an established tale that the town's minute and militia marched under a banner to Concord on April 19. The proposed color in lore has been the "rattlesnake flag" consisting of a coiled reptile with the words "Don't Tread on Me," possibly on a yellow background. However, it is generally accepted that such a banner (either yellow or with thirteen alternating red and white stripes as background, the former known as the Gadsden flag) only appeared on Continental navy ships beginning in the fall of 1775 and early 1776. No evidence exists for its appearance in Concord or with Sudbury units in April 1775.

The final possibility for a flag in Concord on April 19 is the most romantic, perplexing, fascinating and controversial, since its basis in fact relies most heavily on family oral tradition, supposition and theory. This banner is the legendary "Bedford Flag" (still on display at the Bedford Free Public Library in Massachusetts).

According to family lore, Nathaniel Page Jr. was either "elected" to or provided as honorary, the rank of cornet/standard bearer of the Bedford minute company. Upon receiving the April 19 alarm, he is said to have grabbed the ancient cavalry troop flag (allegedly "designated by the minute company as its standard") and marched to Concord. Also told are the tales of the flag, prior to the fighting at North Bridge, being laid down on the ground by Page, where it was played with by town boys and later served as a rallying point for the provincials as they mustered near the bridge. Page is said to have carried the flag not only at the Concord fight, but also into Cambridge and for the entire seven days he was on active

The historic, venerable, treasured color of Page family tradition, the Bedford Flag. *Courtesy of Minute Man National Historical Park archives.*

duty. Both he and the standard then returned home, neither to ever see military service again. Unfortunately, there is a dearth of positive original documentation with which to substantiate these and other stories, even in Bedford primary sources.

Mystery, contradiction and circumstantial evidence, plus a strong desire to believe old tales, seem to surround the Bedford Flag. At first it was thought to be a seventeenth-century cavalry standard that the Three County Troop (1659–77) ordered from London and carried in the wars against the Indians. It has since been shown through fabric analysis by textile experts in Rhode Island and England that the silk was woven in China, taken to England and then perhaps sent to Massachusetts after the seventeenth century. Some of the paint used on the fabric was studied at a Williams College laboratory in 2000 and determined to be the pigment "Prussian blue," which was not formulated before 1704 and was most likely reproduced in England around 1724. Thus, the flag dates most likely from the 1720s at the earliest and perhaps even to the 1740s or 1750s.

Generations of Pages received military commissions in the rank of cornet, responsible for the care and carrying of a unit's flag. The first so named appears to be Nathaniel Page (records reflect at least 1720), who served in a horse troop, followed by his sons, Nathaniel Jr. (records reflect at least 1738) and John, whose commission in the Middlesex County Regiment was dated 1737. There is no documentation to show that Nathaniel Page (called Junior), son of John (thus not actually a Junior; his uncle was Junior), was ever elected or appointed to the rank of cornet. Generally by the 1770s such a military grade no longer existed within provincial minute or militia companies.

Tradition holds that Junior's peers, in recognition of the family's history, assigned him the "honorary" title of cornet. Yet he was listed in Captain Jonathan Wilson's minute company rolls as private. Whereas grave markers of the period generally denoted the highest military rank held by the deceased, that of Nathaniel Jr. (so called) indicated "Mr." His father, uncle and grandfather were all identified on their gravestones as cornets. Finally, there exists no documentation to support the idea that the Bedford minutemen accepted what is known as the Bedford Flag as their "official" standard in 1775. However, none of this information negates the possibility or probability that an old cavalry flag lay dormant in the Page house attic.

More questions arise than are answered concerning this legendary flag and its activities. Why was it carried on April 19 but not at other musters, such as the March 13 regimental drill, weekly gatherings of the Bedford minute company or at town events? Is the arm/dagger/cloud symbol on minute company commander Wilson's tombstone an actual replica of the flag's design or copied from another common source? Why did such a historic, important flag disappear for a hundred years, then abruptly surface at centennial ceremonies in 1875 and again in 1885 when donated to the Town of Bedford? Why would such an ancient, notable flag only develop a storied past in the middle to late nineteenth century? And why would a cornet whose responsibility was to guard and protect—perhaps even with his life—the highly honored colors of a military unit place (according to tradition) the very old, venerable flag on the ground or a stone and allow it to be used as a play object by local boys?

Apparently the core of the flag's story lies in the 1865 Page family reunion, where Ruhamah Page Lane (age seventy-seven) recalled the tales from her father, Nathaniel (called Junior, son of John), of his carrying the standard in 1775 at Concord. Even here confusion arose, as John Page had a brother, Nathaniel Jr. (son of Nathaniel), who was a cornet but not associated with the Concord fight. In 1885, Ruhamah's nephew, Cyrus Page (who was also the grandson of Nathaniel Page, called Junior), donated the flag that had been in his care to the Town of Bedford. It has been rightfully treasured and displayed ever since as an ancient artifact. Cyrus made his donation while explaining that a member of the family on the memorable April 19, 1775, had carried the standard as "the flag of the minutemen."

Perhaps most disappointing in this Bedford Flag puzzle is the complete lack of any primary source evidence that might help to substantiate in any manner that the standard appeared at North Bridge or in the field at all on April 19. Not a single mention of it is made in the myriad of diaries, letters, eyewitness accounts and depositions—British or provincial, civilian or military. Even Bedford materials that might shed a positive and truthful light on the subject are silent, or at least undiscovered as of yet. Had such an unusual standard appeared on the field, without doubt some officer or soldier on either side would have taken notice and surely have put the astonishing sight into writing. It would have been a most unusual vision in 1775 for a militia or minute company of the provincials to carry colors, and would very likely have raised immediate Redcoat concern that a provincial horse troop was nearby.

Several flag books, such as one by Admiral George H. Preble—*History of the Flag of the United States of America* (1872 and 1880)—either make no mention of the Bedford Flag or indicate that probably no colors were carried on April 19, 1775. Other volumes make passing note of the flag, but regarding its presence at Concord or the truth of its April 19 tales simply use such qualifiers as "local belief" or "no documented proof," while still referring to the age of the standard and the respect that it deserves.

Major Lemuel A. Abbott, whose ancestor Moses Abbott as senior lieutenant supposedly took command of the Bedford minute company after Captain Wilson's death, stated in *Descendents of George Abbott of Rowley, Mass.* (1906) that he felt it absurd to think that a one-hundred-year-old flag could be carried on April 19. Interestingly enough, another Bedford family oral tradition notes that Private Edward Stearns took over command of the Bedford minute company after Wilson's death due to the facts that he had previous military experience, once held the rank of lieutenant and was related to Wilson by marriage.

Between August 1906 and December 1907, the *Boston Evening Transcript* printed several letters, with the author listed only as "Rockingham," debunking the Bedford Flag legend as absurd and lacking in truth while calling for authenticated proof. Many thought that a "historian" from another town who was upset with the publicity focused on the newly "discovered" flag might have penned these writings. Yet even the newspaper editor stated, "Tradition is not truth" and asked for the names of historians of repute who backed the flag story.

In perhaps one of the most bizarre stories told in relationship to the Bedford Flag, "Rockingham" noted that the standard's design resembled a Brunswick (German) coin in Europe with its mailed arm, sword and background clouds. He stated that after the surrender in October 1777 of British General John Burgoyne's army at Saratoga, New York, the Brunswick allies under the command of General Friedrich Adolf, Freiherr von Riedesel were imprisoned in and near Boston. While it was thought that the regiment's colors had been burned to avoid capture, in fact they were secretly sewn into personal clothing of the prisoners as a means to save and protect them. The general and his wife, Freifrau Frederika, had hoped to take the flags with them on their move from Massachusetts to Virginia.

Being quartered at Winter Hill, not far from Bedford, Rockingham suggested that deserting Germans might have taken one silken regimental flag in their custody to nearby Bedford for protection or for some other reason, such as bartering. The suggestion was that "somehow" the flag passed into the Page family from the Germans. This was an extremely odd, speculative explanation of the Bedford Flag, how it came by its design and how it arrived in Bedford.

In point of fact Freifrau von Riedesel did assist in the saving and secreting to Cambridge of the regimental colors of the Germans. However, according to her writings *Berufs Reise nach America*, with the assistance of an honorable tailor the flags were sewn into a mattress and sent with an officer who smuggled them through the American lines into the city of New York, thus saving them for return to Brunswick.

In the final analysis regarding the historic Bedford Flag, what can be stated with certainty is that a Nathaniel Page, called Junior (son of John), was with the Bedford minute company in Concord on April 19, 1775, and that the family had in its possession hidden away for many years an ancient flag. Currently the flag is also believed to be the oldest complete, solely American flag in existence. In Long Island, New York, there appear to exist fragments of a late seventeenth-century New England pattern flag that belonged to the Fifth Regiment Massachusetts Militia, which is still being studied.

While Bedford Flag supporters will look at the controversy over the standard's appearance at North Bridge in 1775 and say, "Why not, if you want to believe," at present there exists no factual primary information to support the banner having appeared at the Concord fight. Reverend Ezra

Modern Bedford minuteman crossing North Bridge with a replica of the storied Bedford Flag. *Photograph by Dennis Dostie, MMNHP volunteer.*

Ripley in his 1827 *History of the Fight at Concord*—admittedly a hometown view of April 19—provided some new depositions, interviewed as many living participants as he could find and mentioned that two members of Wilson's Bedford minute company were still alive, but made no mention of a flag. Hopefully it will be to other historians, researchers or family trunk cleaners to answer the many questions surrounding the Bedford Flag. The venerable color is deserving of no less.

Thus it appears that the only documented flag present in Concord on April 19 was unfurled atop the liberty pole and destroyed by the arriving Regulars. And, most likely with nothing in his notes and papers documenting the contrary, Emerson's "their flag" was but poetic imagery or necessary rhyme ("flag unfurled" and "round the world"... two controversial phrases) and the term did not refer to a specific banner at the North Bridge fight.

Abbott, Major Lemuel A. *Descendants of George Abbott of Rowley, Massachusetts*. Boston: T.R. Marvin & Son, 1906.

Brown, Abram E. *Beneath Old Roof-trees*. Boston: Lee & Shepard, 1896.

———. *Flag of the Minutemen April 19, 1775. Its Origin and History*. Bedford, MA: Bedford Historical Society, 1894.

Brown, Louise K. *Wilderness Town*. Bedford, MA: Minuteman Publications, 1968.

Fischer, David Hackett. *Paul Revere's Ride*. New York: Oxford University Press, 1994.

Hitchcock, Barbara. *The Bedford Flag: A National Treasure*. Kirkwood, MA: The Friends of the Bedford Flag, Inc., 1998.

Hurd, D. Hamilton. *History of Middlesex County*. 4 Vols. Philadelphia: J.W. Lewis, 1890.

Kehoe, Colonel Vincent J-R. *We Were There*. Chelmsford, MA: issued by the author, two parts, 1974, 1975.

McDonald, Sharon Lawrence. *The Bedford Flag Unfurled*. Burlington, MA: DSA Printing & Publishing, Inc., 2000.

Sabin, Douglas. "Facts and Legends Associated with the Battle of April 19, 1775." Unpublished manuscript. Concord, MA: Minute Man National Historical Park, 1995.

Tragic Act Begets Revenge and Propaganda

It was a tragic, momentary and questionable act committed by a young man in the emotional aftermath of the Concord North Bridge fight, but both the incident and its perpetrator, who was long shrouded in silence, would have a profound impact on subsequent events, at least on April 19, 1775. Numerous writers avoided, misrepresented, misunderstood or distorted the importance of what often was referred to as "the incident"—perhaps in order to protect historical image.

As the Regulars fled the bridge, Colonel James Barrett's colonials pursued them but a short distance. According to Reverend William Emerson's account, a wounded British soldier, left behind, attempted to rise up and was assaulted by a young fellow going to join his countrymen. Acton's Thomas Thorp noted that the culprit, "not under the feelings of humanity, barbarously broke his [soldier's] skull" with a small hatchet. The sight horrified Thorp.

Ensign Jeremy Lister, among the British troops returning from the search of Barrett's farm, came upon his comrade and wrote, "4 men…killd who afterwards scalp'd their eyes goug'd their noses and ears cut of, such barbarity execut'd upon the Corps could scarcely be paralelled by the most uncivilised savages." Five other Redcoats declared seeing the wounded man with the skin over his eyes cut and also the top part of his ears cut off. As word spread among the British troops in Concord that the colonials were scalping and mauling the dead and wounded, attitudes turned from fear to contempt and hate.

Lieutenant Colonel Francis Smith, commanding the Concord expedition, reported to Lord Hugh Percy and Royal Governor General Thomas Gage

White, believing he is in mortal danger from a wounded British soldier, uses his axe to dispatch the attacker. *Photograph by Richard Stevenson.*

that "after the bridge was quitted, they scalped and otherwise ill-treated one or two of the men who were either killed or severely wounded." Gage wrote in his summaries, "One scalped, his head much mangled and his ears cut off, though not quite dead…a sight which struck the soldiers with horror." Rumors even circulated that eyes had been forced from the dying soldier's sockets. What actually occurred may only be known to the victim, the young "attacker" and possibly Reverend William Emerson. At his nearby parsonage during the incident, the minister apparently spoke to the perpetrator immediately after the fact. The Reverend later acknowledged the fateful axe blow, but insisted that the soldier was neither scalped, nor his ears cut off, but that he did languish for hours before expiring.

Various explanations for the cause of this deed have been advanced. The culprit was "half-witted" (twentieth-century academic source); excited and inexperienced; startled by the soldier and acted out of fear; or acted to end the soldier's suffering (perhaps at the Redcoat's insistence). Other possibilities put forth in explanation included that the victim was trying to drown himself in a water puddle and begged someone to kill him, had thrust at the young colonial with his bayonet, causing a defensive reaction, or was attempting to escape capture. Any mitigating circumstances that existed for sure were known directly only by the perpetrator and the soldier.

The British military and media publicized the incident, perhaps to motivate their soldiers, for propaganda purposes and/or in order to influence public opinion. The colonials chose to ignore it, possibly due to embarrassment, fear of reprisals, failure to appreciate its importance or a notion that it would blemish a historic cause. Provincial authorities hesitated to confirm that the act had occurred, but in response to a Boston newspaper story offered assurances and even had the burial detail testify that "neither of those persons [two dead soldiers buried at the bridge] were scalped nor their ears cut off." Concord historians Dr. Reverend Ezra Ripley, Lemuel Shattuck and George Tolman ignored the incident completely and may not, for various complex reasons, have believed the name they heard to be the culprit. Reverend Joseph Thaxter, of Westford, Massachusetts, a bridge fight participant, remembered the hatchet incident in 1824 and that the soldier had made a thrusting gesture at the young provincial. Well into the twentieth century, British historians continued to write of the scalping and ear-cutting episode.

Contrary to a traditional, long-held belief, the name of the young axe culprit, according to extensive research by Aryeh Finklestein of Newton, Massachusetts, was not purposefully and secretly passed along for generations by word of mouth. It has been acknowledged that Ammi White, born about 1754 in Acton and a member of Captain David Brown's Concord minute company in 1775, was the perpetrator. White may have been an apprentice for cabinetmaker and carpenter Joseph Hosmer and possibly performed work on Reverend William Emerson's parsonage near North Bridge in 1769–70.

Emerson, apparently having spoken to White immediately after the act, told the tale (if not the name) during an interview with visiting historian Reverend William Gordon of Roxbury, Massachusetts, who addressed the incident in a letter and several books. Emerson failed to describe the event in his own April 19, 1775 diary entry. He must, however, have informed family members, because years later, ninety-year-old great-granddaughter Phebe Ripley Chamberlain wrote of the incident in *Diaries and Letters of William Emerson*, mentioning White by name, and noted that Emerson told Gordon that White showed "great concern for its having happened." She also described "a young fellow of twenty-one...named Ammi White, came along, hatchet in hand...looked at the two British soldiers. One was not quite dead, and as he stirred, White killed him with blows to the head." There exists an idea that Emerson may have had reason to remain somewhat quiet—at least publicly—regarding White's incident.

Gordon, in his 1775 narrative, expressed concern that exaggerated portrayals of the "incident" (scalping, ears cut off, eyes gouged out) would be written by "some malevolent pen" in order to horrify readers and reflect badly upon "the fanatics of New England." He concluded, however, that no British soldier was so mistreated and that he explained the "real fact" as he received it from Emerson. Gordon never mentioned White by name.

As late as 1932, Concord historian Allen French interviewed an elderly woman who was reluctant to mention the axe wielder's name, and thus neither did he. Stories abounded that the person was a wood-chopping chore boy of the Emersons or their African servant Frank. The former did not exist and family members exonerated the latter.

Though perhaps he might have been troubled by the incident to some degree during his life, White's true sentiments appear to have been revealed in 1807. He confided to a Concord friend, Charles Handley, that in fact he had struck a wounded Redcoat with an axe immediately following the April 19, 1775 North Bridge fight. He further explained that he thought the soldier was trying to stand and under the circumstances, he did what was expected. White felt that his actions were right and was very surprised at the negative reactions that he later encountered.

Ammi survived the war, was married by Reverend Ezra Ripley to Mary Minot on August 12, 1788, had five children and purchased the Minot family's East House (current section of the extant Colonial Inn) in Concord center. He and his family lived there from 1789 to 1799. White was a highly successful cabinetmaker who hired two or three men in his shop and even provided clock cases for such well-known clockmakers as Joseph Mulliken. One of these, possibly made for the Masonic Corinthian Lodge of Concord (chartered 1797), is on view at the Concord Museum.

White sold his residence to Jean "John" Thoreau (grandfather of Henry David) in 1799 and moved to Westmoreland, New Hampshire, where he died in 1820 at age sixty-six. Nathaniel Hawthorne, having heard the axe story from poet and writer James Russell Lowell, wrote of it in *Mosses from an Old Manse*. He brooded over White's life and how the bloodstain must have tortured his soul. There is no evidence that White harbored such soul-searching feelings, but such concepts are entirely consonant with Hawthorne's writings.

The British troops returning to Boston remembered the "scalping" with fear, anger and a desire for revenge. This, coupled with civilian hostility in Boston and the perceived cowardly tactics of the colonials along the retreat route from Concord to Charlestown, led to bloody reprisals and undisciplined acts (house burnings, killing of unarmed men, bayoneting of wounded and dead colonials) by the Regulars, especially in the village of

Menotomy (present-day Arlington, Massachusetts). Lord Hugh Percy's relief column had been informed of the "scalping" and Royal Governor General Thomas Gage later used it to offset atrocity charges against his own troops.

Thus did an inauspicious, tragic incident near North Bridge that involved a little-known militia private on April 19, 1775, have major implications on later military actions and propaganda efforts by the British army.

NOTE: Astoundingly, even in 2005, the White incident was retold and referenced by a political magazine in the reporting of alleged prisoner abuse by American soldiers in Iraq.

Emerson, Amelia Forbes, arr. *Diaries and Letters of William Emerson 1743–1776.* Concord: privately printed, 1972.

Fischer, David Hackett. *Paul Revere's Ride.* New York: Oxford University Press, 1994.

French, Allen. *The Day of Concord and Lexington.* Boston: Little, Brown and Company, 1925.

Gordon, Reverend William. "An Account of the Commencement of Hostilities Between Great Britain and America in the Province of Massachusetts Bay, May 17, 1775." In *American Archives*, 6 vols., edited by Peter Force, Vol. II, 625–31. Washington, D.C.

———. *The History of the American Revolution.* 2 Vols. Philadelphia, 1789.

———. *The History of the Rise, Progress and Establishment of the United States of America including an Account of the late War and The Thirteen Colonies from Their Origins to that Period.* 4 vols. London, 1788.

———. "Letter to a gentleman in England, May 17, 1775." *Journal of American History* 4, no. 1: 65–72.

Kehoe, Colonel Vincent J-R. *We Were There.* Chelmsford, MA: issued by the author, two parts, 1974, 1975.

Murdock, Harold. *The Nineteenth of April 1775.* Boston: Houghton Mifflin Company, 1925.

Joseph Thaxter
Minister of the Lord at the Bridge

Watchmen upon the walls must not hold their peace—they must cry and not spare, must reprove for what is amiss, and warn when danger is approaching.
—Reverend Moses Parsons, A Minister's Duty, *1772*

I am sorry to say that no body of men are so extremely injurious to peace and tranquility as the clergy. They preach sedition openly from their pulpits.
—Lord Hugh Percy, Boston, 1774

Behold, God himself is with us for our Captain.
2 Chronicles 13:12
—Reverend William Emerson, Concord, March 13, 1775

As the storm clouds of conflict darkened the April 1775 sky, it was no secret that the Congregationalist ministers were for the greater part passionately supportive of liberty and freedom from England's oppression.

Revered by their flocks, local clergy intertwined religion and politics with a frequent, fiery (and lengthy) pulpit rhetoric. For these men of God, civil government and principles of Christianity were joined, and long before the Declaration of Independence was penned they preached the right to life, liberty and property. In addition to spoken and written words used to espouse their beliefs, many ministers sought personal actions, often joining Committees of Correspondence or Safety. For at

Reverend Thaxter looks to his horse being saddled and prepares to ride to Concord in response to the alarm. *Photograph by Dennis Dostie, MMNHP volunteer.*

least one clergyman, even more was required—the taking up of arms and confronting the oppressor.

Joseph Thaxter, born April 23, 1742, was the son of a deacon and farmer. Too poor to afford college, he saved $5, enough to purchase a Massachusetts lottery ticket, and won $500, which paid his way to a 1768 Harvard degree. He was licensed to preach in 1771 and, while looking for a permanent church position, he filled several pulpits as a guest preacher. By 1775 he became embroiled in a Westford, Massachusetts controversy that pitted the first minister (elected 1727), Reverend Willard Hall (accused of being a Tory), against a patriotic populace. Thaxter agreed to preach on a trial basis and his sermons did not disappoint.

Upon receiving the alarm that the king's soldiers were on the road to Concord, Westford's minute and militia companies prepared to march some eleven miles. Anxious to respond, Lieutenant Colonel John Robinson, second in command of a Middlesex County militia regiment, sped by horse to Concord followed by an enthusiastic Thaxter. Dressed in the black cloth of office, the minister carried not only the word of God but also reportedly a brace of pistols—one in each pocket.

In a letter to Reverend Ezra Stiles of Newport, Rhode Island (later president of Yale College), Thaxter described arriving above the North Bridge and seeing some three hundred Regulars, three companies of which remained in place to prevent the colonials from crossing. "Our people" stood on the high ground within 450 yards. In a break with traditional accounts, Thaxter later noted that Colonel James Barrett, feeling his age, turned command over to Robinson, who fired up Major John Buttrick and the others, causing them to follow his lead in a march to the bridge. Some Westford tales even noted that Robinson, possibly alone or at least at the same time as Buttrick, shouted the order for the provincials to fire on the king's soldiers.

In an 1824 letter recording his eyewitness account, Thaxter stated, "We had then no certain information that any had been killed at Lexington; we saw the British making destruction of the town...proposed to advance to the bridge." As the column, including the minister, marched a murderous volley from the Regulars was received. "Our people then fired over one another's heads being in a long column, two and two: they killed two and wounded eleven." No mention was made of Thaxter's exact location in the ranks or whether he fired his pistols.

Like many others after the engagement, Thaxter paused for sustenance, breakfasting with the Reverend William Emerson, whose parsonage was (and still is) hard by the North Bridge. He then joined his late-arriving townsmen, marched to Meriam's Corner and chased the king's soldiers back to Charlestown. The next morning, so the tradition is told, he allegedly captured two Redcoat stragglers coming from a swamp.

Thaxter's military exploits continued on June 16. He proceeded with Colonel John Robinson's militia regiment as a chaplain and amateur surgeon to Breed's Hill, only to face once again Redcoat fire on the next day.

Although offered the Westford church pulpit permanently in January 1776, he declined, and on January 26 was appointed to be one of the first Continental army chaplains (joined in July by friend Reverend Emerson). From 1776 to 1779 Thaxter served in Providence, Rhode Island; Fort Washington, New York; White Plains, New York; Trenton, New Jersey; Lake George and Fort Ticonderoga in New York. He received a wound that caused a permanent limp and the end to his military career.

The embattled minister finally settled down on November 8, 1780, and became pastor of the Edgartown church (Martha's Vineyard, Massachusetts) after having preached in Hingham, Massachusetts, and being elected to the state House of Representatives. He was married twice—first to Molly Allen on October 12, 1781, and then following her untimely death in April 1802, to Ann Smith on July 24, 1803. Both wives were from Edgartown.

Thaxter entered the nineteenth century still wearing the large white wig and tri-cornered hat fashionable in an earlier time, yet he still commanded respect. As one of the last surviving chaplains of the Revolution, he helped lay the cornerstone for the Bunker Hill Monument. He died quietly on July 18, 1827, having lived a tumultuous life.

In an 1824 letter that for the first time explained his roles in and views of the events at Concord (April 19) and Breed's Hill (June 17) in 1775, Thaxter extolled the actions of officers and men. He called for "a decent monument at Concord Bridge, where the first spark was struck, doing no more honour to Robinson and Buttrick then they richly deserve." He added, "I have lived in obscurity on this island [Martha's Vineyard], and never thought myself of importance enough, and capable of doing justice to a historical account of the transactions of the memorable 19th of April."

Reverend Samuel Cooke, minister in 1775 of Menotomy village, sermonized, "We cannot indeed expect to be saved, but in the way of duty, and in a prudent, manly resolute defense of our rights, dearer to us than our lives." And so did a common man of the cloth stand and act with uncommon conviction in a time of need and crisis, only to fade back to obscurity while serving his country and his God.

French, Allen. *The Day of Concord and Lexington*. Boston: Little, Brown and Company, 1925.

Hodgman, Reverend Edwin. *History of the Town of Westford*. Lowell, MA: Morning Mail Company, 1883.

Hudson, Frederick. "Battle of Concord." *Harper's New Monthly Magazine*, May 1875: 778–804.

Shipton, Clifford K. *Sibley's Harvard Graduates 1768–1771*. 18 vols. Massachusetts Historical Society, 1975.

Thaxter, Reverend Joseph. "Letter from an Old Soldier." *U.S. Literary Gazette* 1 (November 30, 1824): 264.

Legacy of the Daughters of Liberty

In the telling of our colonial history, it is common to find little mention of women and their roles, especially in defining moments, for it is a time when the ladies are neither expected nor allowed generally to make decisions or act in pivotal situations. Yet surrounding the April 19, 1775 events in Massachusetts, the daughters of America's liberty were not only visible but active participants as well.

From the beginning, it might have been that the actions of two particular women were major factors in the fight at Concord's North Bridge that led to revolution. Tories and Patriots alike suspected Margaret Kemble Gage, the American-born wife of Boston's royal governor and military commander General Thomas Gage, of committing espionage. It was supposedly whispered that she was having marital difficulties, and harbored hopes that her husband's actions would not be the cause of bloodshed as hostilities increased between England and the provincials.

Thus, it is not difficult to understand why—without any evidence concerning either matter—many thought that she may have been the "spy" who was privy to confidential conversations at the governor's home and office, and who "leaked" specific word of the Concord expedition to Dr. Joseph Warren of the Sons of Liberty. This information set in motion the provincial alarm system that mustered minute and militia companies and led directly to the events of April 19. Detractors of this theory note that specific telltale actions by the British military and the need for numerous officers to be aware of the upcoming expedition were what resulted in the breakdown in secrecy.

In Concord, as word of the Regulars' approach spread, folks, particularly women and children, gathered what belongings they could and fled for safety. At age seventy-one and infirm, widow Martha Moulton remained in her house and, when requested, provided water and whatever sustenance she had to the tired and hungry king's soldiers. During a search of the village, the Redcoats found numerous wooden items, including gun carriages. These were tossed into a pile and set afire next to the Town House, causing dark smoke to rise. Martha begged the officers to have the flames extinguished, and when the roof caught fire, she stood by with a pail of water. Again she yelled for assistance before the building and others in town were lost. There appears to be no truth to the tale that black powder was stored in the Town House attic that would have galvanized the soldiers into taking action to forestall a possible explosion.

Martha's exhortations finally led the king's soldiers to toss water on the flames, which in turn created large, billowing clouds of smoke that rose above the town. When seen by the provincial forces mustered above North Bridge, it caused them to think the town was being destroyed and so they marched toward a confrontation and history. On February 4, 1776, old and destitute, Martha petitioned the Great and General Court of Massachusetts and was granted a bounty (three pounds) for her service to the public and private good on April 19.

Women, many of whom had children in their arms or clinging to their aprons and clothes, enacted various acts of bravery. Those heroines who lived along the Regulars' route of march gathered family items of worth and fled to the woods, relatives' homes or other places of safety. At the parsonage in Concord, the minister's wife, Phebe Bliss Emerson, fainted from shock upon hearing that Redcoats had entered town. She recovered sufficiently to assist in the comforting of frightened families seeking refuge and solace under the roof of the Lord's preacher. Meanwhile, she looked after her own little ones, fretted about her husband's welfare and watched from her second-floor window the events unfolding at North Bridge.

Dorothy (Mrs. Amos) Wood, when her South Bridge home was searched by the soldiers, saved military stores from discovery by indicating that a locked room harbored frightened women. It was thus left unopened by the Redcoats. Hannah Barron (also Barns or Burns), a barmaid living with the family of tavern keep Ephraim Jones, protected the Provincial Treasurer Henry Gardner's chest of money and important papers by blocking the soldiers' entrance to the room, claiming that it and the trunk were her personal belongings. The Regulars were under orders to molest no persons or personal property.

Abigail Wright, wife of a tavern proprietor, was said to have secreted the First Parish communion silver in basement soap barrels to avoid theft. The same tale was attributed to Susanna (Mrs. Jeremiah) Robinson, who supposedly remembered the silver, dashed to the church, gathered the items and then rushed to hide them in her chimney foundation soap barrels. She then defiantly barricaded her door against the Regulars' intrusion.

Other interesting Concord tavern tales survived to be passed through generations of family. Lydia Taylor, whose husband Daniel owned the tavern business operated by Amos in the so-called "Wright Tavern," helped wait upon British officers on the morning of April 19. Frightened and confused, she placed several musket balls in her apron pocket in an attempt to hide them. While making change for one officer, she mistakenly brought forward several of the balls. When asked what she intended to do with them, her reply was said to have been, "Sir, I would use them in a flintlock if I had one."

Meanwhile, Amos's thirteen-year-old daughter Lovina was also working in the tavern. Among other things, she recalled that her mother Abigail saved the church silver. In 1825 at age sixty-three, she also recalled that one officer she served—believed to be Major John Pitcairn—stirred his drink with a "bloody finger" and proclaimed that he "hoped he should stir the Yankee blood so before night." Some believed Lovina Wright Farrar was mistaken and that more likely it had been Lieutenant Colonel Francis Smith who made the oft-quoted remark.

Rebecca Barrett, wife of Concord's militia colonel, helped hide military stores and equipment in the garret of her farmhouse and in the nearby Spruce Hollow woods. Unlike many of her peers, she chose not to flee, noting that she was "too old [fifty-eight] to worry about losing much more" and she wished to protect both her home and her family from harm. When Captain Lawrence Parsons's companies of Regulars arrived at her house near mid-morning, she provided food and beverage but refused to supply spirits. Noting that it was God's word that she should feed her enemies, payment by the Redcoats was rejected. The king's officers then tossed coins into her apron, as the story went, which she announced were "the price of blood."

As the soldiers began to pile a few discovered items to burn, Mrs. Barrett chided them about setting the barn ablaze and thus they moved the materials into the road. When her son Stephen blundered into the house and the name Barrett was announced, soldiers thought that he was the colonel. He was quickly seized for transport back to Boston. Mrs. Barrett again interceded, corrected the misunderstanding and had her son released. The Regulars departed the farm, having found little of value, and while they were treated respectfully, it was sternly so. Following the fight at the bridge, Rebecca's last acts of the day were tending to the wounded provincials.

Melicent Barrett (right with scissors) and other Concord girls roll black powder cartridges that will be used soon by provincials against the king's soldiers. *Photograph by Richard Stevenson.*

Another Barrett woman, Melicent (Milliscent or Meliscent), young and attractive at age fifteen and the granddaughter of Colonel James and Rebecca, had one day tricked a flirting British army officer into showing her how to roll powder cartridges. He used a pair of scissors that on the night of April 18 she and other young women of Concord supposedly used to prepare cartridges that were most likely fired against the Regulars at North Bridge and during the retreat.

For most wives and mothers, it was a time of fear, trauma, uncertainty, terror and often sadness as their husbands and sons went off to fight. While some hid or fled, many remained at home and found some way to contribute to their men's task as best they could. Lydia Mulliken of Lexington watched her fiancé, Dr. Samuel Prescott, ride off, joining Paul Revere and William Dawes to warn Concord citizens of the British threat. Meanwhile, her brother Nathaniel joined Captain John Parker's militia company on the Lexington Common. During the enemy's return from the encounter in Concord, they paused near Lydia's house and, when they left, burned it and the family clock shop to the ground.

In Lincoln, Mary Flint Hartwell's day began around 1:30 a.m. on April 19 when she heard Dr. Prescott's night alarm, handed her baby to a frightened servant and ran a distance in the dark to warn the commander of the town's minute company, Captain William Smith, of the approaching danger. Accounts differ as to whether she remained in hiding at the house after her minuteman husband departed or fled to her brother's residence a distance away—which was the more likely. Regardless, her home received damage from the retreating Redcoats, including musket ball holes. The next day she and her children followed, for a short distance, an ox cart that held five dead Regulars who were being taken to the Lincoln Burying Ground. Mary had sympathy not only for the men who died so far from home but also for their families in England.

From her home next to Lexington Common, Ruth Harrington watched her husband Jonathan standing with Parker's company as he was struck by a Redcoat's musket ball. He crawled to their house doorway and died at her feet.

Hannah Davis in Acton, like many wives, had said farewell to husband Isaac as he marched off to Concord with his minute company. With four sick young children and a bad-omen owl found in the house (as the story is told), intuition warned her that she would never see him alive again. As he disappeared, Isaac called a request that she take good care of the children. Later that day, following the action at North Bridge, Hannah realized she was a widow when his corpse was returned to the house.

In the town of Menotomy, also known as West Cambridge (Arlington), supply wagons lagged far behind Lord Percy's relief column that was marching westward to meet the beleaguered Colonel Smith, and were ambushed by a group of old men. Some six Redcoat guards fled toward Spy Pond in an attempt to save themselves and disposed of their weapons into the water, then surrendered to the protection of a fifty-eight-year-old widow "Mother" Ruth Batherick. As the story was told, she relinquished the prisoners to a local militia captain with the parting comment, "If you ever get back, you tell King George that an old woman took six of his Grenadiers prisoner." Word of this event reached England, where the opposition press noted, "If one old Yankee woman can take six Grenadiers prisoner, how many soldiers will it take to conquer the Colonies in America?" Batherick died in an almshouse in 1795 and her tale was supported by noted men of the time. One local historian later claimed that she was "an old black woman" but no evidence exists to support that statement.

Many women, especially during the Regulars' unruly retreat, sought to save themselves, their children and their homes under dire circumstances. Hannah Adams of Menotomy, the wife of Deacon Joseph, had five children in her house and lay in bed with her eighteen-day-old baby girl. When soldiers burst into the room, she supposedly exclaimed, "For the Lord's sake, don't kill me!" She was allowed to leave the house with the baby, but her other five children were hiding under the bed. The soldiers set the house ablaze and while they pilfered communion silver were suddenly addressed and threatened by a nine-year-old boy. After the Redcoats fled, the children extinguished the fire.

Mrs. Samuel Butterfield returned to her Menotomy home after the king's soldiers had passed through the village on their way to Charlestown. To her astonishment she discovered a bleeding, dying British officer, Lieutenant Edward Hull of the Forty-third Regiment, in one bed and a wounded provincial believed to be a Mr. Hemenway from Framingham in another. She provided care to both and while the latter survived, the lieutenant died ten days later and the body was sent to Boston. A neighbor had threatened to kill the officer, and accused Butterfield of being a Tory sympathizer. She defended her actions and Lieutenant Hull with the exclamation, "Only cowards would want to kill a dying man."

Personal loss was common this day. In Bedford, eleven-year-old Alice Sterns (later Mrs. Moses Abbott) with her mother Lucy and sisters Rachel, age seventeen, and Susanna, age thirteen, spent April 19 at home making cartridges. These items were sent along with food to the men in the field, who included father Edward and brother Solomon. Later she recollected, "I suppose it was a dreadful day in our house and sad indeed for our brother, so dearly loved, never came home." Solomon stayed with the army in Cambridge and on May 18 died of a camp disease at age nineteen.

Some women went to extraordinary lengths in liberty's cause, as was the case in the town of Pepperell, Massachusetts. Prudence Cummings Wright was the sister of one Patriot and two Tories. She espoused the colonial desire for appropriate freedoms.

During the months leading to April 19, Prudence suffered a double tragedy. First she lost Mary, a six-year-old daughter, to fever on July 1, 1774. Eighteen days later she gave birth to a baby boy named Liberty, who then died suddenly at age seven months, on March 11, 1775. At the time she had six other children, including twins, and gave birth four more times, including in 1778 to another baby she named Liberty.

Having taken time to grieve and recover as best as possible, Prudence watched as her husband David, a militia private, marched off with the other local men toward Concord with his company under Captain Josiah Sartell. She realized there was no longer time for self-pity. Rumors abounded that Regulars were murdering families and committing other "atrocities," which fed the people's fears, especially now that most of the men were gone. There were also tales of spies and Loyalists carrying dispatches from Canada to Boston through the Groton, Hollis and Pepperell area across the local bridge. Knowing that such information might result in harm to their husbands, fathers and brothers, the towns' ladies decided to act.

The women formed a "military" company, wore their men's clothing and armed themselves with whatever firearms, pitchforks, clubs and weapons they could find. Strong, resolute, religious and courageous, Prudence Cummings Wright was elected their captain, and she selected Sarah (Hartwell) Shattuck as her lieutenant. The choice made sense, as the two were neighbors and Sarah's husband Job was first lieutenant of David Wright's militia company. Together all the women set about patrolling the town and most especially the bridge over the Nashua River.

It was not long before two riders approached the bridge's patrol and were challenged. As the story is told, one of the riders was Thomas Cummings, who recognized the voice of his sister Prudence and fled. The second man attempted to cross the river. Captain Leonard Whiting, a Tory, was surrounded and captured by the women, who found in his stockings dispatches for Boston that related to British army troop deployments and reinforcements. The prisoner and his papers were turned over to appropriate officials and so ended the exploits of the women's "military" company.

Aside from Wright and Shattuck, none of the other thirty or so women's names seem to have been recorded. However, they all shared the payment of seven pounds, seven shillings and six pence for their night's work. On December 22, 1824, "Captain Prudence" died at age eighty-four. "Lieutenant Sarah" passed away in 1798, but not before seeing her husband rise to the rank of captain, only to be convicted of treason after the Revolution, sentenced to hang and eventually pardoned for his part as a leader of Shays' Rebellion.

Such exploits would set the stage for later female military heroines, including Margaret "Captain Molly" Corbin, wounded and captured in 1776 at the Battle of Fort Washington, New York; Mary "Molly Pitcher" Ludwig Hays, at the 1778 Battle of Monmouth, New Jersey; Deborah Sampson (Continental army soldier 1782–83, disguised as a man, "Robert Shurtleff"), who was wounded twice, discovered, released from service and granted a pension; Sibyl Ludington, age sixteen, who rode and alarmed the New York countryside when Danbury, Connecticut, was attacked in 1777.

Thus from its earliest days, America's struggle for liberty and freedom was waged and greatly influenced by America's women as well as its men. Whether they took up trades, operated the farms and shops, provided knitted clothing and blankets or looked after and protected the family alone, women were not inferior to men in courage, resourcefulness, determination or patriotism. Such a legacy from liberty's daughters should never be overlooked, ignored or taken lightly, for among future generations, it would be repeated.

Butler, Caleb. *History of the Town of Groton, Including Pepperell and Shirley*. Boston: Press of T.R. Marvin, 1848.

Drake, Samuel Adams. *History of Middlesex County, Massachusetts*. Vols. I and II. Boston: Estes and Lauriet Publishers, 1880.

Faran, Palmer. *Heroine of the Battle Road*. Lincoln, MA: The Cottage Press, 1995.

Fischer, David Hackett. *Paul Revere's Ride*. New York: Oxford University Press, 1994.

French, Allen. *The Day of Concord and Lexington*. Boston: Little, Brown and Company, 1925.

Hunter, John P. "No Foe to Freedom Should Pass That Bridge." *The Journal of the Colonial Williamsburg Foundation*, Summer 2006.

Kehoe, Colonel Vincent J-R. *We Were There*. Chelmsford, MA: issued by the author, two parts, 1974, 1975.

Scudder, Townsend. *Concord: American Town*. Boston: Little, Brown and Company, 1947.

Shattuck, Lemuel. *History of the Town of Concord to 1832*. Boston: Russell, Odiorne, and Company, 1835.

Shattuck, Mary L.P. *Prudence Wright and the Women Who Guarded the Bridge*. Wheeler Print, 1899. Reprint, Daughters of the American Revolution, 1979.

Wheelwright, Andrew. Public address. Publications of the Colonial Society of Massachusetts 7. Cambridge, MA: University Press, 1900.

A Matter of Color
Slaves and the Two Fights for Freedom

On the morning of Tuesday, October 25, 1774, the First Provincial Congress met in Concord to address the desperate state of the colony and its relations with England. Concerns had already been voiced that delegates were "conscious at the same time of no alternative between the horrors of slavery or the carnage and desolation of civil war."

Early on, Mr. Joseph Wheeler brought forward to Dr. Nathaniel Appleton a letter directed to him "purporting the propriety, that while we are attempting to free ourselves from our present embarrassments, and preserve ourselves from slavery, that we also take into consideration the state and circumstances of the negro slaves in this province." This message was read aloud and a committee appointed to consider the matter. "After some debate thereon, the question was put, whether the matter now subside, and it passed in the affirmative." Thus the issue of black servitude was sidestepped.

On the eve of a revolution that had among its goals to avoid "the horrors of slavery" and maintain the natural rights of man, it seemed a contradiction that some twelve Concord families owned slaves or servants. This peculiar institution seems to have been a part of the town scene at least as early as the 1660s, when its founder Reverend Peter Buckeley's grandson, Major Peter Buckeley, Esq., owned a Negro and an Indian servant. In 1708, Antoner (a Negro son) was born to Antoner and Margarett (both Negroes) residing in Concord. At most during the eighteenth century, slaves owned in town numbered no more than twenty-one men, women and children.

Better treated than their counterparts in some colonies, Concord slaves or servants could exercise certain rights and under provincial law were supposed to be meaningfully employed and educated by their owners, especially in the ways of God and religion (sometimes ignored). Often they were an integral part of the family economic unit in which they served, living within their owner's house. They could become freemen (no longer bonded to an owner for life) through an owner's last will and testament, by military service or by raising enough personal monies to purchase their freedom. A custom of the time was to assign slaves names chosen from Greek or Latin classical literature (Cato, Plato, Caesar) or related to the servant's past history, so that the son of a tribal king might be called Prince.

Historically, law prohibited blacks from serving in militias (being armed), but that was often ignored during most eighteenth-century American colonial wars, due to manpower shortages. With the master's consent, a slave could enter the military, but was rarely allowed to do so because of his economic value on the farm, at the shop or around the house. Investigations of these matters and any aspect of the lives of people of color are difficult at best due to the scant records that were maintained on them unless they were noteworthy in act and deed for some reason.

A common fear among whites was that armed slaves might revolt. In 1768 this feeling was reinforced when a British officer, Captain John Wilson, was arrested and charged in Boston for inciting blacks "to fight against their masters." The 1771 Great and General Court of Massachusetts voted to ban slavery in the colony, but the civilian royal governor vetoed the legislation. Yet in 1774 some Boston slaves supposedly offered their military service to the new Royal Governor General Thomas Gage if, in return, he would agree to free them. Other rumors suggested that Tories were arousing the slaves who were out on the roads to kill Patriots. Fears spread in such towns as West Cambridge/Menotomy, Ipswich and Stoneham. Even Abigail Adams in September 1774 wrote of the growing concern about a slave uprising conspiracy. And, as their minute and militia companies marched to the April 19 alarm, citizens remaining behind in Framingham heard rumors that Negroes (which Negroes?) were coming to massacre them and gathered arms for protection. Such was the hysteria of the time.

During the fall and winter of 1774, blacks (including Concord's), with very few exceptions, most likely did not drill with town militias or minute units. But as spring approached, bringing with it the increased threat of armed conflict with England, volunteers were sought, which in some instances included blacks. While no official records list Negroes as serving in Concord's companies by 1775, a notation on one muster roll seemed to indicate Philip Barrett (Colonel James Barrett's slave, purchased at age eleven in Boston, 1771) present at a militia drill. Since he was only fourteen, it is more likely that he only accompanied the colonel but did not directly serve. This may also have been the case with several other Concord slaves.

In addition to Barrett, other town slave owners in 1775 included Tory and former slave trader Duncan Ingraham (owner of Cato); Town Meeting moderator Dr./Colonel John Cuming (owner of Brister); militia Captain George Minot (owner of Caesar); muster master Samuel Whitney (owner of Casey); Reverend William Emerson (owner of Frank); Deacon Simon Hunt (owner of Caesar Robbins); and Tory and religious activist Dr. Joseph Lee (owner of Cato). While these slaves may not have fought at North Bridge, many did serve later in the War for Independence either as militia or Continental line soldiers.

A few records document the role of blacks fighting against British Regulars alongside their white townsmen on April 19. Prince Estabrook, a thirty-four-year-old Negro, was servant to Benjamin Estabrook (selectman, justice of the peace, Town Meeting moderator) and a member of Captain John Parker's Lexington militia company. Whether out of loyalty to his master, to serve in his master's place or to earn his freedom, Prince was on the Lexington Common when the king's soldiers arrived. In the skirmish that occurred at sunrise, he was wounded and most likely remained off the field of conflict for the remainder of the day. However, from June 1775 through 1782 he served in Boston and Cambridge, at Fort Ticonderoga and elsewhere in New York, both with the militia and with the Continental army, Third Massachusetts Regiment. It is not known exactly when he was given his freedom, but the 1790 Massachusetts census listed Prince in Benjamin Estabrook's family as a non-white freeman.

Also involved with Parker's company was Eli Burdoo, "a man of color" whose name appears on the muster roster on April 19, and a Silas Burdoo, noted as "non-white" who claimed to have been a volunteer with Parker at Lexington and who served from Breed's Hill (June 1775) until the war's end (1783) and earned his freedom.

According to tradition, Caesar Jones (with owner Lieutenant Timothy Jones), Cambridge Moore and Caesar Prescott were possibly in the Bedford ranks at Concord's North Bridge as volunteers. Caesar Bason, perhaps owned by James Burns, represented Westford and marched with Captain Jonathan Minot's company. He later served and died at Breed's

Framingham's Peter Salem tells of his days fighting against the king's Regulars. *Photograph by Dennis Dostie, MMNHP volunteer.*

Hill in June. Numerous towns counted black men in the ranks of their companies that marched to "the alarum" but unfortunately few muster rolls of the town militias at that event exist, or if they do, men of color were omitted.

One intriguing Concord traditional story of April 19 centers on Cato Ingraham, servant of merchant and former slave trader Duncan Ingraham. Cato stood at his owner's house, hands behind his back, as the Regulars approached. A soldier (Major John Pitcairn has been mentioned), believing that he had a weapon, pointed a pistol to his head and demanded his arms. Unflustered, Cato raised his left arm and then his right, noting that those were the only arms he possessed. He later achieved his freedom, married, built a house and was mentioned by Henry David Thoreau in his famous book *Walden.*

Heroic tales abound of the deeds performed by local people of color on April 19. Many are of oral tradition, and some were written soon after the events occurred. For example, Menotomy's Cuff Cartright ignored British soldiers' warnings, accepted a bribe to remain silent and then rode through town anyway to spread the alarm. There was mulatto David Lamson, a French and Indian War veteran who (some say) led the "old men of Menotomy" in their capture of British army supply wagons.

Captain Simon Edgell's Framingham minute company responded quickly to the alarm and engaged the retreating Redcoats near the Brooks farm in Lincoln. In the ranks were Jeffrey Hemenway, a mulatto who had served in the French and Indian War and eventually gained his freedom, and Peter Salem, a black slave who was freed by his owner to enlist and was traditionally thought to have killed British Major John Pitcairn at Breed's Hill in June 1775. Salem served throughout the Revolution and lived a free life afterward.

Although perhaps they were not involved at the bridge fight, Concord's blacks distinguished themselves in later military service. Philip Barrett served in July 1775, enlisted in Captain Samuel Heald's company in September 1779 and completed a six-month tour at West Point, New York (1780–81). He never returned to Concord, perhaps in great part due to his bondage/servitude being continued until he reached age thirty (nine more years) as specified in owner Colonel Barrett's 1779 will.

Brister (Cuming) Freeman, owned by Dr./Colonel John Cuming, served under Colonel John Buttrick at Saratoga, New York (1777), saw British General John Burgoyne surrender, enlisted again in 1779, earned his freedom, returned to Concord, settled and married. Perhaps among his reasons for entering the military were cruel tricks and insults by local men and boys that made him passionate and quarrelsome, and his extremely strong desire to become a freeman. He was often confused (even by Henry David Thoreau in his book *Walden*) with the Lincoln slave of John Hoar, called Brister Hoar, who with his master's permission served at Saratoga in the place of Joshua Child Jr. Brister Hoar changed his name, either during military service or at least by 1791, to Sippio or Sippio Brister and resided in Lincoln until his death on November 1, 1829. He was buried in Lincoln's Old Precinct Burial Ground near the grave of five British soldiers who died on April 19.

Caesar Minot, servant of Captain George Minot, served three months (1775–76), signed for a three-year enlistment (1779) and returned to settle in Concord at the war's end. Casey Whitney, owned by the town's muster master Samuel Whitney, dreamed often of returning to his home and family in Africa from whence he had been snatched at age twenty. Henry David Thoreau reported such in an 1858 journal entry. Often harassed, especially by his owner's sons, Caesar tossed an axe at them once following a snowball-throwing incident. He was chastised with ugly slurs by his owner, which led to his fleeing into the wilderness of the Great Meadows and eventually enlisting in the army. Upon war's end, he was freed and returned to Concord.

Pompey Blackman (also Pompey Fortune or Pomp Freeman) entered the military from Concord after April 19, 1775. He served various enlistments from Boston to Fort Ticonderoga and Saratoga, New York; from Valley Forge, Pennsylvania, to the Battle of Monmouth, New Jersey; and finally to Rhode Island, where he was discharged in 1780. In 1782 as a freeman residing in Lexington, Massachusetts, he was baptized in the Congregational Church before moving to Jaffrey, New Hampshire, where he died in 1790. Caesar Robbins, owned by Simon Hunt, resided not far from North Bridge and, though not apparently in the Concord fight, served in the army through the battle at Saratoga, New York, in 1777. Being freed by 1790, he married twice and built a house in Concord that still stands (324 Bedford Street) in an area settled by men of color.

Caesar Augustus, so the story is told, was wounded and taken prisoner at Charlestown (near Boston) around dusk on April 19. He was returned to his owner, Mr. Tileston of Dorchester, on June 5 when prisoners were exchanged between the provincials and British authorities. Lieutenant Frederick Mackenzie, Twenty-third Regiment, Royal Welch Fusiliers, noted in his diary that the last casualty of the day was "a Negro (the only one [who] was seen to fire at the King's troops) was wounded…near the [Charlestown] Neck."

Existing records (though incomplete and sketchy) indicate that at least some 40 men of color, or about 1 percent of the day's total provincial response, were involved in the "alarum" and fights of April 19, 1775. At Breed's Hill/Bunker's Hill on June 17, 1775, the men of color engaged totaled at least 150, or 5 percent of the total colonial force. Many were killed or wounded in liberty's cause. General George Washington, commander in chief of the Continental army, supported the enlistment of men of color into the army's ranks while the Continental Congress and many states opposed the idea. However, over 5,000 of the total American army soldiers during the War for Independence could be noted as men of color.

At the same time that many Concord citizens opposed slavery and supported its abolition, a 1773 petition seeking redress and freedom was prepared by a group of Negroes and presented to the Great and General Court. Consideration was tabled, and Governor Thomas Hutchinson noted that his instructions from England made support of the request impossible. Negroes of Bristol and Worcester Counties on March 24, 1775, petitioned the Worcester County Committee of Correspondence for help in obtaining their freedom. At the County Convention of June 14, 1775, it was noted, "We abhor the enslaving of any of the human race…and particular of the Negroes in this county." Help in any way possible was offered, but not forthcoming in reality.

Another Negro petition in 1777 led to the Massachusetts legislature drafting an anti-slavery bill but the Continental Congress caused it to be abandoned, as it would harm interstate relations. When the British army captured black men, they were imprisoned or sold into slavery in the West Indies. Attempts at offering freedom for service or general freedom instead met with such fierce Southern Loyalist opposition that the ideas were abandoned.

The Massachusetts State Constitution was ratified by 1780, but only after a Declaration of Rights was added through the persistence of John Adams, stating (after a change) that all men were "born free and equal." With that phrase as a basis, the State Supreme Court, after a two-year case, decided in 1783 in favor of a runaway slave and his protector. Thus after numerous attempts had failed, slavery was legally ended in Massachusetts for all practical purposes.

The military role of Concord's slaves and freemen and their fellow men of color in Massachusetts and throughout the colonies from the early days of the conflict, and right through the Revolution, must neither be ignored nor diminished. Service in two fights for freedom saw them eventually cleanse the evils of slavery in Massachusetts, raise the hopes of a people, even where attitudes and discrimination continued, and earn for themselves the rights and status of freemen, all the while bringing independence for and liberty to a new nation.

According to the epitaph of Concord's most famous slave, John Jack, written by Tory Daniel Bliss in 1773, "God wishes man free, man wills us slaves. I will as God wills; God's will be done."

Elliott, Barbara K., and Janet W. Jones. "Concord: Its Black History 1636–1860." Unpublished manuscript, Special Collections, Concord Free Public Library, 1976.

Greene, Lorenzo Johnston. *The Negro in Colonial New England 1620–1776*. New York: Columbia University Press, 1942.

Gross, Robert A. *The Minutemen and Their World*. New York: Hill and Wang, 1976.

McManus, Edgar J. *Black Bondage in the North*. Syracuse: Syracuse University Press, 1973.

Piersen, William D. *Black Yankees*. Amherst: University of Massachusetts Press, 1988.

Quintal, George, Jr. "Patriots of Color: 'A Peculiar Beauty and Merit.'" Report for and published by the Boston National Historical Park and Minute Man National Historical Park, National Park Service, Department of the Interior, February 2002.

Sabin, Doug. "The Role of Blacks in the Battle of April 19, 1775." Unpublished manuscript. Concord, MA: Minute Man National Historical Park, 1987.

Trumbull, Joan. "Concord and the Negro." Vassar College paper, Special Collections, Concord Free Public Library, Concord, MA, 1944.

Support from Our British "Cousins"

In recent history it has been observed that in time of need, our British "cousins" in the United Kingdom have come to the support and aid of their American "relatives." Interestingly enough, and little known or remembered, is that the historic precedent for such was solidified in April 1775 during America's fight for independence from the British government.

Following the "Lexington alarum," eyewitness depositions and a narrative graphically depicting the "attack" and "atrocities" by the British soldiers against Massachusetts citizens (of British extraction) were quickly gathered by the Provincial Congress and sped by ship to London. With propaganda and the winning of British hearts and minds as the goals, these documents arrived well in advance of any official announcements from the royal governor or British military commanders and they indeed had their intended impact.

As a consequence, numerous groups gathered in London and across the English countryside to voice distress over the reports from Massachusetts. Their actions and opinions were contrary to established government policy, while expressing a sense of kinship with their American "relations" thousands of miles away and sympathizing with their cause. One "Patriotic Society" wrote to Mr. John Adams, whom they had earlier elected a member in 1773, expressing a desire to defend rights on either side of the ocean since Britain at that time had limited individual rights and representation. This organization supported local political candidates for office who would "try to restore America's right to taxation by representation of her own choice" (*Lloyd's Evening Post*, August 24–26, 1774).

Another "radical" establishment, the Constitutional Society (later changed into the Society for Constitutional Information), consisted of dissidents from the society known as Bill of Rights Supporters. Internal disputes among these groups influenced the 1773 Parliamentary elections, causing the disenchanted to form even more organizations. Many of these allied themselves with the principles of their American "brothers" and counted among their numbers people from the Essex-Suffolk border and East Anglia, who had a history of supporting self-governance and rights. They also could relate to and sympathize with embattled "cousins" residing in far-off villages with place names familiar to them, such as Dedham, Newton, Sudbury, Haverhill, Boston and Lincoln.

Arrival in London of the Lexington/Concord fight accounts was met with such responses as "the sword of Civil War is…most universally believed to have first been drawn by General Gages [*sic*] troops" (William Lee, June 1775). Considered to be anti-government measures, the publishing of these early reports in London led to extensive and vigorous legal prosecution of the printers. Yet former minister and pamphleteer John Horne (later Horne-Tooke) and others of the Constitutional Society signed a newspaper insert on June 5, 1775, calling for cash donations to aid the colonists. The *Essex Gazette* reported that some £100 were raised. Publishers found guilty of seditious libel were fined £100. Mr. Horne, supporting the cause of liberty, was eventually tried in court, imprisoned for a year and fined £200 in November 1777. Still the opposition to American policy fostered letters to King George stating, "a civil war commenced in America by your Majesty's Commander-in-Chief…nothing to expect from America but gazettes of blood, mutual lists of their slaughtered fellow subjects."

It should be noted that Horne's written newspaper appeal was for "the relief of the widows, orphans, and aged parents of our beloved American fellow-subjects, who faithful to their character of Englishmen, preferred death to slavery, were, for that reason only, inhumanly murdered by the King's Troops at or near Lexington and Concord." The Constitutional Society had already elected to advance £100 sterling to the cause, paying such to the firm of Browne and Collinson on the account of Benjamin Franklin, Esquire. The Massachusetts Council formed a committee on October 25, 1775, to receive the monies through Franklin from "charitable persons in England for the relief of wounded, widows/children of the slain."

Support for Massachusetts continued throughout the summer of 1775. The pro-American London Association, considered subversive by the government, called upon "true friends of liberty and country to rally before the colonies were alienated or lost" in a September 1775 "Declaration of Grievances." As the spirit of opposition continued to grow, the livery organizations of London proposed giving £2,000 of city revenue to the New England Rebels. However, due to the prosecution of Horne, this idea was never made public. The Middlesex electors at their annual "Festivity to Liberty" on July 27, 1775, toasted "all those American heroes who like men nobly prefer death to slavery and chains"; Mr. John Hancock and John Adams "and all our worthy fellow-subjects in America, who are nobly contending for our rights with their own"; and General Israel Putnam, who "risques his life in support of a good government." Thomas Joel, secretary of the London Association, wrote a funeral oration for the American victims of Lexington and Concord.

British Loyalists and the opposition contended with one another on both sides of the ocean throughout the American war. The former raised money to "suppress rebellion and sedition," as stated in the king's August 23, 1775 proclamation that placed in jeopardy all who aided or abetted the American Rebels and also assisted the soldiers and "the widows of brave men fallen to defend Constitutional Government of this country." The latter collected funds to support the colonials' fight and better the conditions of some 924 harshly treated American Rebels (including Colonel Ethan Allen) incarcerated in British prisons. In the winter of 1778 the London Common Council raised £5,000, as reported in the *London Evening Post & Public Advertiser.* The opposition also stood against army enlistments—especially by coercion—to obtain men to serve in America. "By denying to the King and Lord North's administration the national unanimity that they sought in the face of colonial rebellion, the pro-Americans (of London) justified their own assertion that the American War for Independence was in fact a Civil War," wrote John Sainsbury in *Disaffected Patriots*, 1987.

Prior to any of these activities of support, numbers of high-profile Englishmen lent their views, voices and political clout to the colonial cause. A prime example was Irish-born, Trinity College–educated Edmund Burke, who had been elected to the House of Commons in 1765. A writer, intellectual and orator of note, he defended America on the question of taxation by Parliament and helped obtain the repeal of the Stamp Act. He addressed provincial taxes again in 1774 and spoke in 1775 to the need for England to take the first step toward reconciliation with the colonies. Burke opined that Americans were of a special nature and needed to be governed accordingly with consideration. Once war exploded onto the scene, Burke expressed concerns in a letter to the sheriffs of Bristol (whom he served in Parliament) that England's movement to suppress American liberties could eventually have an impact on liberties in Bristol.

John Wilkes, member of Parliament and staunch supporter of fairer treatment of the American colonies, also feared that rights would be lost in

Edmund Burke addresses the British House of Commons in support of the cause of the American colonies. *Reprinted from* The Public and Domestic Life of the Right Hon. Edmund Burke *by Peter Burke, Esq., 1853. O'Neill Library Boston College.*

Britain if the colonies failed in their cause. Thus he found ways to secretly funnel financial aid to the Rebels for several years. He started a newspaper, the *North Briton*, which attacked the king and his policies. Wilkes was arrested and held in the Tower of London on charges of seditious libel and was removed from Parliament. He fled to France in 1768, but returned to be reelected to Parliament—much to the anger of the king. He railed against the 1774 Coercive Acts, becoming a hero to the Americans, who sent him gifts, while some in England saw him as evil incarnate. Despite this—or perhaps because of it—he became the lord mayor of London in November 1774.

In 1776 Philadelphia, a drama by Styner and Cist entitled *The Fall of British Tyranny or American Liberty Triumphant* was performed and dedicated to "Lord Boston" (General Gage). Other characters in this play included "Lord Patriot" (Wilkes), "Bold Irishman" (Burke), "Judas" (Governor Hutchinson), "Lord Hypocrite" (Lord Dartmouth), "Lord Catspaw" (Lord North), "Mr. Caper" (General Burgoyne) and "General Washington" (who personified all the American officers and soldiers).

Wilkes continued his support of the colonies and was assisted by his brother-in-law, George Hayley, who was also a politician and commercial agent in London for John Hancock. Following the British army defeat at Saratoga, New York, in 1777, Wilkes dangerously stated, "I am sorry that 800 valiant English and Germans were killed in a bad cause, in fighting the best constitution on earth." Such support from a small, vocal constituency in Great Britain in some measure bolstered American morale and aided eventual victory and independence for the colonies.

In the two centuries removed from the April 19, 1775 events at Lexington and Concord, America came to the aid of its mother country in two world wars and other crisis situations. It was, therefore, not surprising to find our British "cousins" rising in support of our cause against a common foe following September 11, 2001, when once again freedoms, liberties and a way of life were threatened. Over the many years, the peoples of "old" England and New England have found and shared common ground and have remained one in "kinship," spirit and history.

Clark, Doris M. *British Opinion and the American Revolution*. New Haven, CT: Yale University Press, 1930.

French, Allen. *The First Year of the American Revolution*. Boston: Houghton Mifflin Company, 1934.

Lossing, Benson John. *The Pictorial Field-Book of the Revolution*. 2 Vols. New York: Harper & Brothers Publishers, 1850.

Minutes of the Bristol Convention 1774. Publications of the Colonial Society of Massachusetts 1. Cambridge, MA: University Press, 1894.

Phillips, Kevin. *The Cousins' War*. New York: Basic Books, Perseus Books Group, 1999.

Sainsbury, John. *Disaffected Patriots: London Supporters of Revolutionary America 1769–1782*. Kingston: McGill—Queen's University Press, Canada, 1987.

Intolerable Papists Influence a Revolution

That there should be liberty of conscience to all Christians (Papists excepted).
—Concord Town Meeting letter on rights and liberties, January 19, 1774

Many a minuteman and militiaman at North Bridge on April 19, 1775, harbored a historic resentment toward the pope and his Church. While their Puritan ancestors settled Massachusetts and Concord with a goal of purifying the Anglican Church, they also were determined to avoid all connections with Catholicism. Spiritual beliefs as well as governance were in the hands of the church members (Congregational), not bishops, popes or kings.

Anti-Catholic sentiments had always been manifested in Concord as well as in Massachusetts in general. Town founder Reverend Peter Bulkeley (1636–1659) warned of the "scarlet whore of Rome." Questionable rumors surfaced that King James, who appointed the unpopular Sir Edmund Andros as governor, harbored a desire to eliminate Protestantism and move England (and thus New England) closer to Rome's control. Both king and governor were eventually deposed. Concord's Reverend Joseph Estabrook (1667–1711) preached against anything popish and once, after using a communion plate inscribed with papal insignia ("IHS," a cross and three nails of the crucifixion), saw it smashed to pieces by his deacon. (The plate can still be seen at the Concord Museum.)

Other activities reflected the ill will of colonists toward the Roman Church. Many towns celebrated Pope's Day, which memorialized the failed 1605 Catholic plot to blow up Parliament. In Boston, people drank, burned effigies of the pope and priests, paraded through the streets and often rioted—the worst occurrence being in 1764. An early 1700s influx of persecuted Protestant French Huguenots to Boston helped to further inflame hatred for Catholics. So too did atrocities committed by Catholic France's "savage" allies during the French and Indian Wars (1754–63). When the British government—in response to the destruction of taxed tea by a Bostonian mob in December 1773—instituted the "Intolerable Acts," which included the shocking Quebec Act of 1774 giving French Canadian Catholics and their priests equal religious rights, the New England colonists reacted angrily.

At this time in history, European Catholic nations were experiencing a power struggle among kings, governments and the Church, with the Society of Jesus (Jesuits) serving as a focal point. The Age of Reason had already reached its height (1748–63) and the Rationalism of Enlightenment continued to catch the imagination of people. Meanwhile, Rome's traditional power was waning, being challenged by rulers, aristocratic governing bodies and new popular attitudes. The latter included such irreligious philosophies as Jansenism (corruption of human nature, inability of will to do good, Christ died for predestined people not all men), Gallicanism (favored local bishop and temporal power over papal authority) and Erastianism (state superiority in ecclesiastical matters).

Against this assault on Rome's authority there stood the staunch, conservative, tradition-based Jesuits, whose allegiance was directly to and in defense of the Pope, as "grenadiers" of his guard. The society, while garnering popular support, had amassed much property, wealth and power, which led many to view them with suspicion. Jesuits were also labeled as masters of intrigue and thus feared as a threat by the heads of state. Detractors charged the society with disobedience to the church and a lust for material wealth. Perhaps its real sin was supporting the concept that authority of any ruler came from the people and not God. Jesuits were—in the words of the day—"disturbing the peace" (especially of the enemies of the Church).

The Jesuits' actual "enemies" were the Bourbon royal families ruling most Catholic states; European Freemasonry that challenged many tenets and control of the Roman Church and chastised the society while supporting Enlightenment views and reform; and secular-minded Roman bureaucrats, both lay and clergy. With high-ranking Masonic statesmen advising kings, the Jesuits' existence was in jeopardy, yet they met in conclave in May–June 1758 and elected to stand fast to their ways and beliefs. Pope Clement XII

(1730–1749) had condemned Freemasonry and ruled that any Catholic joining the organization would be excommunicated.

However, attacks against the society increased and its dismembering came swiftly, beginning with Portugal (1759–61), where arrests of priests were made, property and wealth were confiscated and Jesuits were banished to Italian states by the Portuguese government. Then France used a court case in 1762 that was upheld by Parliament and supported by King Louis XV and his queen, Madame de Pompadour, to expel the order as incompatible with the welfare of the state. Next, Spain (1767) was an immense agitator against and persecutor of the society, followed by Naples and Parma, each of which removed Jesuits from within their borders. Supporters for the Jesuits were hard found.

The pending election of a new pope in 1769 gave the Catholic rulers an opportunity to influence the cardinals into electing a person who would definitively act against the society, de facto sanctioning their previous judgments against the Jesuits. Interference, intrigue and unwarranted pressuring relative to the papal election were unprecedented. Professing a desire for reconciliation between Rome and the kings and peace within the Church, in order to combat irreligious world philosophies, a cardinal who also was a Franciscan friar agreed that a pope had the power to extinguish a religious order if done properly. This friar became Pope Clement XIV, who by 1772 began closing Rome's Jesuit seminary, homes and churches.

Reluctantly, Clement also issued the so-called *Dominus ac Redemptor*, a papal brief—not a bull, which would be irreversible—dated July 21, 1773, that stated, "We hereby suppress the Society of Jesus...ordered abolished... for all eternity." It referenced historic precedent, the need for Church unity and Jesuit quarrels, but never cited any formal charges or improper actions. Neither did the decree place any aspersions on rules, individuals or orthodox teachings within or by the Jesuit Order or its members. The Order in turn never blamed the pope for the situation, but obeyed and disbanded, and in some instances reorganized under the names of several new religious organizations.

Pope Clement was a supporter of the Society of Jesus and its priests, but he was also weak of character and lacking in diplomatic abilities. Broken-hearted, he died some fourteen months later, according to physicians due to overwork and a lengthy illness, though the Spanish authorities and others claimed death was due to poisoning by the Jesuits.

Several nations, such as Switzerland, Poland (for a while) and Austria, allowed the Society of Jesus to continue functioning marginally. England under King George III, who had formed a relationship of sorts with Pope Clement, benignly allowed the order to exist in the unique situation

CLEMENS XIV.

Clemens XIV.

Ad perpetuam rei memoriam.

Zum ewigen Gedächtniße.

Dominus, ac Redemptor noster JESUS CHRISTUS Princeps pacis a Propheta prænuntiatus, quod hunc in mundum veniens per Angelos primum pastoribus significavit, ac demum per se ipsum antequam in cælos ascenderet, semel & iterum suis reliquit discipulis; ubi omnia Deo Patri reconciliavisset, pacificans per sanguinem crucis suæ, sive quæ in terris, sive quæ in cælis sunt, Apostolis etiam reconciliationis tradidit ministerium, posuitque in eis verbum reconciliationis, ut legatione fungentes pro Christo, qui non est dissensionis Deus, sed pacis, & dilectionis, universo Orbi pacem annuntiarent, & ad id potissimum sua studia conferrent

Unser Herr und Erlöser Jesus Christus, der von dem Propheten vorher verkündigte Fürst des Friedens, den er, als er in diese Welt kam, zu erst durch die Engel den Hirten bedeutet, und endlich durch sich selbst, bevor er in den Himmel auffuhr, wiederholltermalen seinen Jüngern hinterlassen; hat, nachdem er alles mit seinem göttlichen Vater versöhnet, und was sowohl auf Erde, als in den Himmeln ist, durch das Blut seines Kreuzes beruhiget hatte, auch den Aposteln das Amt der Versöhnung übergeben, und das Wort derselben in sie geleget, damit sie als Gesandte Christi, der kein Gott der Zwietracht, sondern ein Gott des Friedens und der Liebe ist, der ganzen Welt den Frieden verkündigten, und alle ihre Mühe und Arbeit dahin verwendeten,

A 2 da

Initial page of the 1773 papal decree suppressing the Jesuits. On the left is the original Latin and on the right, the German translation. *Courtesy of Loyola University Chicago Special Collections.*

of a corporate discipline. However, its Jesuit Province, which included Wales, Pennsylvania and Maryland, was dissolved. The first English Jesuit college founded in France had moved to Liège under the protection of the principality prince-bishop where the priests lived as Jesuits in everything but name. By 1778 Rome recognized the college as a pontifical seminary. England already had a precedent of not obeying edicts from Rome, as when Pope Gregory XIII replaced the Julian calendar with the Gregorian calendar in 1582 and Parliament did not accept the change until 1752.

Non-Catholic Frederick II of Prussia felt powerful enough to defy Rome and the Bourbons, while appreciating that some four hundred Jesuits had years before come under his domain with the partitioning of Polish lands. He thus allowed the order to exist for another three years (1776) before dissolving it into the "Priests of the Royal Schools Institute," a secular group.

Empress Catherine (Katerina) II "The Great" of Russia, who was also not Roman Catholic, rejected the suppression outright. The partitioned Polish land in 1772 combined with Lithuania territory—all of which became part of Russia—had brought to her country some two hundred Jesuit priests who had done much for the cultural, educational, scientific and spiritual wealth of her court and people. Catherine decided that if she did not receive the papal emissary with the official document from Rome, she could not and would not obey it. In January 1774 she ordered the Jesuits to ignore the brief. Threats of trade restrictions by Bourbon Catholic nations made the empress more resolute. Soon, these religious conflicts would have influence in anti-papist Massachusetts and Concord.

As this religious, social and political drama played out in Europe, during March 1775, Irish Catholics among the British army ranks in Boston were permitted to celebrate St. Patrick's Day. Much to the horror of the town's citizens, the army "parole" or password of the day was "St. Patrick," with a countersign of "Ireland." Unfounded rumors accused Royal Governor General Thomas Gage of being a papist with designs on converting the colonies to Catholicism by the sword. It seems that George III and Pope Clement XIV had formulated a working relationship in 1772 respecting each other's stances. This situation had heightened hopes for emancipating British Catholics who had suffered religious-based restriction of rights for many years.

Following events at Lexington and Concord, an American army invaded Canada with the aim of making that British territory the fourteenth colony. Congress hoped to enlist French Canadian support for this expedition, but the Catholics neither forgot nor forgave Protestant New England's intolerance, or its negative reaction to the Quebec Act. Left with little Canadian assistance, the under-manned American forces were eventually defeated, and Captain Thomas Theodore Bliss, along with a number of his Concord men, was captured and imprisoned for the remainder of the war.

British Parliament declared the colonists Rebels and set about mustering an army to quickly put down this uprising. Negotiations were conducted with Russia to obtain troops to augment British Regulars in America, but Empress Catherine declined, electing to remain neutral. England hired Prussian/German mercenaries instead.

As the Revolution progressed, France was persuaded to ally itself with America, following the October 1777 victory by the colonials at Saratoga, New York. By September 1778, a French fleet was in Boston Harbor and by June 1780 a French army landed at Newport, Rhode Island. The attitudes of the citizens of Concord and Massachusetts toward papists, by necessity, had to and did begin to change. So as not to offend their new Catholic allies, a prohibition against Pope's Day celebrations was imposed. A Franciscan monk was even allowed to celebrate a secret funeral Mass in Boston (in the basement of King's Chapel) for a French officer killed accidentally in a bread riot.

France and most especially Spain continued pressing the pope to take action against Russia for harboring and aiding the dissolved Jesuit order. Catherine noted that she was mistress of her own house, and allowed the Jesuits to open a new novitiate and elect a series of vicars-general between 1780 and 1783. Quietly, Pope Pius VI gave verbal approval that provided hope for the future of the society. With the Bourbons continuing to agitate, in November 1782 Catherine threatened to abolish religious freedom for the Roman Catholics in White Russia (Byelorussia province from Polish and Lithuanian lands) and convert them to the Orthodox Church. She then indicated the possibility of ending her neutrality relative to the war involving the American colonies and entering the conflict on the side of England. France and Spain, already allied with the Americans, wisely chose to soften their stance and thus kept Russia out of the North American conflict. An American-French victory against the British-German forces at Yorktown (1781) soon led to a peace treaty and independence (1783) for the American colonies.

After 1773, Maryland Jesuit ("defrocked" with the order's suppression), John Carroll, became Rebel sympathizer while quietly remaining a priest. His distant relative Charles Carroll was a statesman and the only Catholic signer of the Declaration of Independence. Following America's independence and a Vatican softening toward the Society of Jesus suppression, John was elected by fellow priests (1789), with papal approval, as bishop to America's twenty-five thousand Catholics in the newly created diocese of Baltimore. After the Revolution he worked tirelessly to have the Society of Jesus reinstated. This goal was finally realized worldwide when Pope Pius VII issued the restoration order on August 7, 1814. In 1816, Thomas Jefferson wrote John Adams, "Like you, I disapprove of the restoration of the Jesuits, which seems to portend a backward step from light to darkness." It seems that these founding fathers were solid men of the Enlightenment's theories and attitudes.

Thus did the intolerable papists and the Society of Jesus, especially its Russian members, play a fateful if indirect role in the American War for Independence in a time when they were "excepted from a liberty of conscience."

NOTE: Irish Catholics helped build Concord's railroads in the 1840s and 1850s; Nathaniel Hawthorne's daughter Rose became a Catholic and founded a hospice religious order; the first public Catholic Mass was celebrated in Concord in 1844; St. Bernard Catholic Church was founded in 1863; and from 1962 to 1971 the Jesuits operated Xavier High School in Concord.

Ahlstrom, Sidney E. *A Religious History of the American People*. 2 Vols. Garden City, NY: Doubleday & Company, Inc., 1975.

Bangert, SJ, Reverend William. *History of the Society of Jesus*. St. Louis: St. Louis Institute, 1972.

Birnbaum, Louis. *Red Dawn at Lexington*. Boston: Houghton Mifflin Company, 1986.

Cordara, Giulio Cesare. *On the Suppression of the Society of Jesus: A Contemporary Account*. Translated and with notes by Reverend John P. Murphy, SJ. Chicago: Jesuit Way, 1999.

Forbes, Esther. *Paul Revere and the World He Lived In*. Boston: Houghton Mifflin Company, 1942.

Scudder, Townsend. *Concord: American Town*. Boston: Little, Brown and Company, 1947.

Teele, John Whittemore. *The Meeting House on the Green: A History of the First Parish in Concord and its Church*. Concord, MA: First Parish, Committee for Publication, 1985.

Irksome Concord Jail and a Parliamentarian Prisoner

I am lodged in a dungeon...black with grease and litter...shut up from the yard... either for my health or the necessary calls of nature...two small windows...gloomy light...season of the frost and snow...corner of the cell, stands a necessary-house... does not seem to have been emptied...a loathsome black-hole.
—Archibald Campbell, Concord Gaol, February 14, 1777

Concord's first gaol (or jail) was built in 1754. The initial purpose was to house French prisoners and their Indian allies who might be captured during the war. There were no "savages" and few Frenchmen, as most were allowed passage elsewhere instead. The two-story facility was made of logs, had four cells, external wooden stairs and a stockade yard for exercise and sanitation. Prior to this time, prisoners were sent to Cambridge or Charlestown (closer to Boston and the nearest jails).

Originally located near jailer Jonathan Heywood's house at the town's center, the jail was moved in the spring of 1770 using tree-trunk rollers and twenty-six pairs of oxen. It journeyed past the millpond and around a corner heading west, and was placed near the old mill in the West Burying Ground area. The new site was on land purchased from Captain Ephraim Jones (builder of the Wright Tavern), who kept a tavern on South Bridge Road. It was common practice to locate jails and taverns in close proximity in order to facilitate the feeding of prisoners. Jones followed Heywood as jailer.

No list of prisoners existed until the events of April 19, 1775, when cells began to fill quickly. By April 25, captured British soldiers, including Sergeant Matthew Hayes and eight privates, were "guests" in the gaol. Several notorious Tories joined them later, namely Dr. Josiah Jones and Dr. Jonathan Hicks, both of whom would escape with outside aid.

Perhaps the most noteworthy prisoner of this period was Lieutenant Colonel (later Sir) Archibald Campbell of Inverneill, Scotland, elected a member of the British Parliament in 1774. Having helped Colonel Simon Fraser raise the Seventy-first Highland Regiment to fight in America, he sailed for the colonies with the unit in late April of 1776. At age thirty-seven and with extensive military experience, he was given command of the Second Battalion and was aboard the transport ship *George*. A horrid storm separated the fleet's ships and Campbell found himself responsible for five vessels and four hundred men. On June 16, after seven weeks at sea, they sighted Cape Ann on the northern Massachusetts coast and the flotilla turned south for Boston Harbor.

Unbeknownst to Campbell, the British royal governor and his military forces, along with many Tories, had evacuated Boston on March 17 and traveled to Nova Scotia. As Campbell sailed his ships past the harbor islands, cannon fire erupted, which he initially took to be a welcoming salute until balls struck his vessels. Suddenly the cannonade was supported by an attack of privateers. After a short engagement, in which his second in command and seven soldiers were killed and another thirteen wounded, Campbell chose to save the remainder of his men and surrender. Congress ordered the officers to be jailed inland, away from the coast and possible escape.

Campbell was initially quartered in a private Reading, Massachusetts residence with twenty-two servants and staff. He quickly became demanding of the populace and a nuisance. In December, following the capture of American General Charles Lee, British officials refused to negotiate a prisoner exchange. That, coupled with rumors that colonial prisoners (including Lee and Colonel Ethan Allen) were being mistreated, led to extreme public dissatisfaction and a demand for redress and revenge. Congress passed a January 6, 1776 resolve changing the conditions of British prisoners, including officers. Safe and close custody with limited privileges became the new standard.

Campbell was transferred to the Concord jail on February 1, 1777, thus beginning a fifteen-month "visit" that included numerous attempts at prisoner exchange, charges of mistreatment and a flurry of complaint letters to General George Washington and Sir William Howe, British commander at New York City. Additionally, these two senior commanders exchanged numerous correspondences on the Campbell issue, and each

A 1777 sketch of the Concord gaol believed to be accomplished by Colonel Campbell or one of his fellow prisoners, John Wilson. *Courtesy of the Concord Free Public Library, Concord, Massachusetts.*

wrote Congress and the Boston Council. In a condescending February 4 letter to Washington, Campbell referred to him as "dictator" and deplored "treatment notoriously dishonorable and inhumane in the annals of warfare." He stated that he lived in a dungeon with wood blackened by grease and the litter of previous criminal occupants, had only two portholes with bars to view the outside, could not go to the yard for the call of nature and was not allowed his servants.

After a reduction in the hostile tone of Campbell's messages, Washington responded that he did not have the power to set aside the edicts of Congress. His Excellency also noted that Congress had informed him that its resolves on prisoner issues would not be changed, but that it did not mean for Campbell to suffer.

A letter from Washington did, however, cause the Boston Council to inspect conditions at the Concord jail in March 1777. At the same time, General Lee wrote a letter stating that he was not being mistreated and neither should Campbell. This led to Campbell being moved to a room in the jailer's tavern and being given use of the yard and one servant. It was during this period that the colonel or a fellow prisoner, James Wilson, accomplished a sketch of the gaol (currently on display at the Concord Free Public Library).

While he acknowledged, in May 1777, the agreeable changes to his living situation, Campbell then proceeded to complain of noise, insults and rowdy guests at the tavern and requested movement to a pleasanter, better provisioned, more livable town, such as Reading, Dunstable or Lancaster. He also demanded the use of two servants, a groom and a cook. Meanwhile, he informed his subordinate officers that he would not allow them to be involved in a prisoner exchange, for it was proper that they should remain with their men in jail.

In August 1777, Washington again approached Howe concerning a prisoner exchange but with no success. By November 6, Campbell was allowed total parole of Concord town limits in return for his word not to escape. He visited shops and homes and was well cared for by the people, jailer and especially Dr. Timothy Minot's daughter, Mrs. Tilly (Mary) Merrick. She nursed a very ill Campbell back to health and years later when her diplomat son, Tilly Merrick, was captured and imprisoned at Halifax, Nova Scotia, the colonel would help gain his release.

Finally on March 30, 1778, orders came for the release of Campbell. He quickly traveled to New York City and on May 6 was exchanged for American Colonel Ethan Allen, a prisoner since his September 1775 capture during the invasion of Quebec.

Colonel Campbell rejoined his Highland Regiment and exacted revenge for his confinement by defeating an American force at Briar Creek and capturing Savannah and Augusta, Georgia, in late 1777 and early 1778. He later became a major general; served as lieutenant governor of Jamaica and governor of Madras, India; was created a knight of Bath; was promoted to colonel in the Seventy-fourth Highland Regiment; and retired to London, where he was reelected to Parliament. He died on March 31, 1791, at age fifty-two and was buried with ceremonies and notable grave markers in the Poet's Corner of Westminster Abbey.

Historian/biographer Charles H. Walcott, while noting in 1898 that Campbell was a "foe" many a year ago during our Revolution, acknowledged that his memory should still be honored based upon his accomplishments. Walcott mused that due to the difficult fortunes of war, it was impossible for Campbell to have enjoyed his stay in Concord's gaol but that later generations should at least regret that the forced residency was not more pleasant or at least less irksome.

As for the jail, after the Revolution it housed Patriot debtors, criminals and dissenters from Shays' Rebellion. In 1788, a new stone facility was built that for one day (July 23, 1846) held Henry David Thoreau for non-payment of his poll tax. The old wooden jail served as a hatter's shop and a stable (1812) before its demise. However, for a small building of minimal importance, the gaol had a most interesting and storied existence in Concord's history, if only for its holding of Sir Archibald Campbell.

Scudder, Townsend. *Concord: American Town*. Boston: Little, Brown and Company, 1947.

Shattuck, Lemuel. *History of the Town of Concord to 1832*. Boston: Russell, Odiorne, and Company, 1835.

Walcott, Charles H. *Sir Archibald Campbell of Inverneill Sometime Prisoner of War In the Jail at Concord, Massachusetts*. Boston: Beacon Press, 1898.

Wheeler, Ruth R. *Concord: Climate for Freedom*. Yarmouthport, MA: Printing and Publishing Production Associates, 1967.

About the Author

The author as Captain William Smith, commander of the Lincoln minute company in 1775, at his house. *Photograph by Gary Wayne Gilbert, marketing communications, Boston College.*

Born and raised in the seaport town of Gloucester, Massachusetts, Mike began his higher education at the U.S. Military Academy and received his degrees at Boston College. Following ten years as a decorated U.S. Army Infantry Ranger captain and Vietnam combat veteran, he returned to BC in 1976, from whence he retired in 2007 as associate dean for student development and a lecturer in history.

Mike currently is a part-time ranger at Minute Man National Historical Park, Concord, Massachusetts (where he was a twenty-year volunteer) and is involved in researching, writing, reenacting, interpreting and teaching relative to the American Revolution, with a focus on the 1770s in Massachusetts, specifically the events on and surrounding April 19, 1775. Debunking and rectifying myths, untruths and revisionism are among his goals. He belongs to numerous reenacting units, both American and French, while serving as historian of the Concord and Lincoln Minute Men; directing the Guild of Historic Interpreters; playing eight period characters; holding memberships in a myriad of historical and genealogical societies, including the Colonial Society of Massachusetts.

An accomplished musician, Mike is the historian, spokesman and percussionist for the internationally known eighteenth- and nineteenth-century group The Jolly Rogues, most recently a major hit in the People's Republic of China. He resides in the "estimable town" of Concord, Massachusetts, but still considers Gloucester "home."

OTHER TITLES IN OUR

MASSACHUSETTS COLLECTION

Lexington, Massachusetts: Treasures from Historic Archives
Richard P. Kollen
$19.99 • 978.1.59629.103.4

The Fish and the *Falcon*: Gloucester's Resolute Role in America's Fight for Freedom
Joseph E. Garland
$34.99 • 978.1.59629.007.5

The *T.W. Lawson*: The Fate of the World's Only Seven-Masted Schooner
Thomas Hall
$21.99 • 978.1.59629.208.6

Lobstering off Cape Ann: A Lifetime Lobsterman Remembers
Peter K. Prybot
$22.99 • 978.1.59629.085.3

A Day in the Life of Hull: You Don't Have to Catch Fish to Go Fishin'
John Galluzzo
$19.99 • 978.1.59629.141.6

When Hull Freezes Over: Historic Winter Tales from the Massachusetts Shore
John Galluzzo
$21.99 • 978.1.59629.099.0